Inside
American
Ballet
Theatre

Inside American Ballet Theatre

INTRODUCTION AND COMMENTARIES BY
Clive Barnes

A Helene Obolensky Enterprises, Inc. Book

Hawthorn Books, Inc.
Publishers/New York

ACKNOWLEDGMENTS

Photographs on pages 31, 33, 34, 35, 36, 37, 38, 39, 40, 41, and 42 are courtesy of the Dance Collection, The New York Public Library at Lincoln Center, Astor, Lenox and Tilden Foundations.

INSIDE AMERICAN BALLET THEATRE

Library of Congress Catalog Card Number: 76–19758
ISBN: 0–8015–4049–6, cloth; 0–8015–4050–X, paper
1 2 3 4 5 6 7 8 9 10

Contents

Foreword
by Justin S. Colin

As a man involved in the world of finance but also one who is dedicated, almost addicted, to the world of the arts, I am especially pleased to have the opportunity to say a few words about my favorite subject, American Ballet Theatre company. The time seems especially propitious, as we begin our two hundred and first year and an even stronger era in the world of dance.

I joined the board of ABT a short decade ago, yet, with the knowledge that I have acquired and the joy that I have experienced, it seems to have been half a century! I have witnessed an incredible growth on the part of this ballet company; it has developed a singular ability to reach out and stimulate, even as it increases the size of, its dazzled audience. The company has expanded the scope of its vision and the excellence of its presentations while providing a display of the most exceptional, world-famous talents.

I feel that our company's approach is truly unique. Particularly attuned to the public's wishes, it endeavors to provide the best available talent from every corner of the world. In the past the American public could expect mere glimpses of a few of the international ballet companies, such as the Royal, the Bolshoi, or the Kirov—all severely limited in the duration of their tours. Now, at least in part through our own touring program and ABT's adroit use of guest stars, audiences in major cities across the country can watch the premier talents of these great companies. Because of its extensive repertory and its magnificently translated classic productions, an ABT season provides excitement as well as variety, with,

for example, Lynn Seymour from the Royal Ballet company joining us overnight to dance the role of Juliet and Richard Cragun of the Stuttgart providing a thoughtful Siegfried to our own Natalia Makarova's bold Odile and vulnerable Odette. During the course of each season many, many unique talents are brought to the United States by ABT to devise brilliant combinations and to partner the magnificent members of our own company. It is from these effective interactions that ABT has obtained its most superlative performances. Although Alicia Alonso, Carla Fracci, and Erik Bruhn are all currently based either in their respective homelands or in their adopted countries, their associations with ABT have been so extensive that one cannot help but consider these artists an integral part of ABT's own family structure.

The goals of ABT are many and varied. First and foremost, however, is our pursuit of excellence. We wish to satisfy the public, giving it, within our resources, the unexpected, always renewed, always improved. The public wants to see great dancing—with productions worthy of the performing talent. ABT endeavors to select and provide programs that showcase the form and particular styles of its dancers, as well as to present full-length productions to illuminate our entire ensemble. Ideally, ABT would love to be able to stage at least one new or revived full-length production per year. Our approach is flexible, as our classic works demonstrate. Dance is our language, freedom is our style. Sometimes ABT may seem abrasive, like a rock musical, but it is contemporary theatre. Its quality derives from every element of each performance. Finally, ABT provides the opportunity for choreographers to premiere new and daring expressions while utilizing the best dancers in the world; during this past year Alvin Ailey, John Butler, Agnes de Mille, John Neumeier, Jerome Robbins, Glen Tetley, and Twyla Tharp were represented with new works.

As it has demonstrated over and over again, ABT delights in inviting dancers from other companies and other countries to join and create exciting combinations and unexpected juxtapositions of talent, such as with the Baryshnikov/Jamison partnering. And ABT welcomes further dance exchanges to expand its own dance horizons. ABT wants to take chances, to experiment; it depends upon flexibility and imagination. Rather than restrict itself to intimate theatres, ABT is looking for large performing centers, both for practical reasons and for space and stage requirements. Where we play is part of what we become.

ABT's future is to be an inspiration for dance. We want to provide the public with the greatest variety of expressions while demonstrating our dancers' unique expertise. Our new *Sleeping Beauty* is only worthwhile if it is a conception that can be realized on stage by dancers who have never lived in St. Petersburg. Dance history up to now has been Dance as Dullsville. The success of ABT lies in that it has become the institutionalized, Americanized evolution of the Diaghilev concept.

Inside
American
Ballet
Theatre

Introduction

The opening of American Ballet Theatre was nothing short of sensational. Its first advertisement in December 1939 announcing a three-week season promised "The Greatest Ballets of All Time Staged by Greatest Collaboration in Ballet History!" Certainly, ballet enthusiasts were led to expect a rather unusual debut.

It is this kind of unlimited vision and scope that has distinguished American Ballet Theatre from its formation.

It must be remembered that at Ballet Theatre's inception the United States had no tradition of a national ballet. Indeed, it had no concept of a national theatre, nor for that matter of a national opera, although over the years the Metropolitan Opera House had in fact functioned in that capacity. For America had none of the traditions of court theatres that were to be found all over Europe, with the sole exception of Britain. Like Britain, America had to build up its national dance companies from scratch. This took a great deal of courage, enterprise, imagination, and, of course, money.

Romantic ballet began to acquire popularity in the United States toward the middle of the nineteenth century. The Austrian ballerina Fanny Elssler made one of her most significant triumphs during her United States tour in 1840. Soon there were home-grown American dancers, such as Mary Ann Lee, who danced *Giselle* with distinction at the Paris Opéra along with her partner, who had the uncompromising name of George Washington Smith and boasted an exceedingly handsome moustache on the stage. All very American.

In 1916 Diaghilev's Ballets Russes gave three seasons in New York, including performances by Vaslav Nijinsky, and, of course, Anna Pavlova made a number of tours in the United States, spreading, wherever she went, the gospel of the dance. However, it was 1933 that proved the turning point in American dance history. That year witnessed the American debut of Colonel de Basil's Ballet Russe de Monte Carlo; it was in a sense the successor of the great Diaghilev company, which had disbanded following the death of its founder in 1929. This company caused the first wave of balletomania all over the Western world. The principal choreographers were Leonide Massine, George Balanchine, and Diaghilev's own first choreographic mentor, Michel Fokine. It was a remarkable company that included earlier Diaghilev stars, dancers such as Alexandra Danilova, Massine himself, and Leon Woizikowski, as well as expatriate Russian dancers, many of them born in Paris and all of them trained in Paris under the post-revolutionary generation of St. Petersburg ballerinas who had set up schools in the French capital. These new dancers included the teen-age ballerinas Tamara Toumanova, Irina Baronova, Tatiana Riabouchinska, and a new male dancer, David Lichine.

Of equal importance in 1933 was the young Lincoln Kirstein's invitation to the almost equally young George Balanchine to come to America and form first the School of American Ballet and subsequently the series of companies that would eventually lead in 1948 to the formation of the New York City Ballet.

While most of the Russian teachers expelled from St. Petersburg or Moscow by the Soviet Revolution ended up in Paris or, in a few cases, London, there were some who came over to America and began to teach the new generation of American dancers. Prominent among them was Mikhail Mordkin, a Muscovite dancer who had previously partnered Pavlova. Having left Russia in 1923, he formed, a year later, a company that performed in the *Greenwich Village Follies*. His major company, the Russian Ballet Company, was formed in 1937, and two years later it became the basis of ABT.

The man who had the idea to form American Ballet Theatre—originally called Ballet Theatre—was Richard Pleasant. An unusual young man, Pleasant was born in 1909 in Denver, Colorado, was educated at Princeton, where he graduated as an architect, and somehow drifted to Hollywood as an artist's representative. In 1937 he came to New York and became manager of Mordkins's Ballet Company. One of the ballerinas of the Russian Ballet and one of the principal backers of the company was Lucia Chase. She had come to ballet comparatively late in her life but had a natural facility and became a ballerina with Mordkin, dancing such roles as Giselle. Pleasant suggested the idea of Ballet Theatre to Lucia Chase and others and finally persuaded everyone concerned that the time had come for some specifically American view of classic dance. The Mordkin Ballet Company soon changed its focus when Mordkin dropped out.

Perhaps important to note at this juncture is the state of American dance at the time. The war in Europe began in September of 1939, and the major expatriate Russian touring companies, which by this time already had their share of English, French, and American dancers and personnel, found themselves for the most part stranded in the United States. Another important factor was the beginning in America of an indigenous dance tradition, which had become known as modern dance.

This parallel dance culture, which was peculiarly American, was over the years to interrelate with and cross-feed into American classic ballet. Modern dance had begun around the turn of the century with Isadora Duncan. While Isadora left no tradition of dance behind her, she did inspire an entire generation to see an America dancing. Among these were Ted Shawn and Ruth St. Denis, who formed the Denishawn School; among their most famous students were Martha Graham and Doris Humphrey. From this school developed an entire network of American modern dance, which was supplemented during the 1930s by the adoption of a German branch, primarily led by Hanya Holm, herself a pupil of Mary Wigman.

America did not have anything it could specifically call an American folk dance, though there was a fascinating variety of ethnic strains in the new nation, many of which had brought along their own specific dance culture. Square dances, for example, had been adapted from various English forms. There was also a very strongly developed form of social dancing, including one that evolved out of jazz. All of these elements in American dance culture were eventually to be encompassed and expressed by the emerging national companies.

Richard Pleasant and Lincoln Kirstein, the originators of Ballet Theatre and New York City Ballet, respectively, maintained different views on how to form a great national company. Kirstein took a cautious, slow, and creative approach, forming initially the School of American Ballet, headed by one of the world's greatest choreographers, George Balanchine. This company began as a fairly modest group that did not attempt to compete with the stars or the glamor of the various Ballet Russe companies that were at that time popularizing ballet in the United States. It was an approach that, unbeknown to either Kirstein or Balanchine, had a great deal in common with the methods used by Ninette de Valois in forming the Sadler's Wells Ballet (now the Royal Ballet, Covent Garden) in London.

Pleasant took a far more flamboyant and pragmatic approach. There must have been much more of the pure entrepreneur in him, for he envisioned a company that would emerge full-fledged, and if not quite as he claimed—the greatest company the world had ever seen—it would be at least be able to match in glamor, quality of stars, and even repertory the Ballet Russe companies that were then so popular in New York. It was an extraordinarily bold move, and one wonders how a penniless young man persuaded so many people to back him.

Pleasant envisioned an organization that would embrace the ballets of all nations and from all times. Old works would be cared for, new works were to be born, everything was to be the best in that best of all possible companies. Such grandiose schemes might have occurred to a European, but only an American would have attempted to execute them, and only in America, particularly perhaps at that time, could one have come so close to success.

Pleasant made a very clever decision that, clever though it was, finally proved impractical: He divided his company into "wings," allocating different choreographers to each. These various wings were classic (Anton Dolin and Bronislava Nijinska); Russian (Adolph Bolm, Yurek Shabelevsky, Michel Fokine, and later, David Lichine and Leonide Massine); American (Eugene Loring, Agnes de Mille, and later, Jerome Robbins and Michael Kidd); Negro (which produced only one ballet, De Mille's *Black Ritual*); Spanish (José Fernandez and, later, Argentinita); and

British (Antony Tudor, Andrée Howard, and Anton Dolin). For dancers the new company drew upon the existing Ballet Company of Mikhail Mordkin and was strengthened by a number of Russian and British stars as well as by the rising American generation. The first performance was presented at the Center Theater in New York, on January 11, 1940, and it was indeed a remarkable beginning.

The dancers for that first season, while not especially famous, did include a new generation of emerging American ballerinas, including Patricia Bowman, Karen Conrad, Viola Essen, and Annabelle Lyon, as well as a number of expatriate Russians, such as Dimitri Romanoff (who has been associated with the company from that first performance until the present day), Yurek Shabelevsky, Adolph Bolm, and that British-born, Russian-by-adoption Anton Dolin. Perhaps of more significance was the number of young dancers in the ensemble who were soon to make their presence felt in American ballet: Miriam Golden, Nora Kaye (who started her career with the company as Nora Koreff until she decided that an American name would be more appropriate), Leon Danielian (today the director of American Ballet Theatre School), Maria Karnilova, Agnes de Mille, Herbert Bliss, and Donald Saddler. By the summer of 1940 these dancers had been augmented by Alicia Alonso, Fernando Alonso, Muriel Bentley, Nana Gollner, John Kriza, and Jerome Robbins.

The opening performance consisted of Les Sylphides; a new "balletplay" by William Saroyan called The Great American Goof, which had choreography by Eugene Loring; and a holdover from Mordkin's Ballet Company, Voices of Spring. The next day the company presented Dolin's production of Giselle with Annabelle Lyon in the title role and Dolin himself as Albrecht.

That first season lasted three weeks. The Center Theater, long since destroyed, had a 3,500-seat capacity, and for the most part, it was sold out. Indeed, had it not been for the fact that Walt Disney's Pinocchio was due to move into the theater on February 4, this premiere engagement would easily have been extended. Pleasant had announced the unusual initial repertory figure of twenty-one ballets, and he actually succeeded in presenting eighteen.

After the first performance John Martin, writing in the New York Times, described the opening as "the beginning of a new era." Walter Terry in the New York Herald Tribune was no less enthusiastic, writing about "the finest performance of Fokine's Les Sylphides that New York has seen in many a season. The master himself in charge of directing it, Les Sylphides emerged the beautiful, breath-taking work that it had not been away from his guiding hand."

During the season there were classic ballets, including the second act of Swan Lake and Nijinska's version of La Fille Mal Gardée, plus works by Dolin, Shabelevsky, Bolm, and Agnes de Mille's work for the black wing, called Black Ritual. The British wing produced some of the most important works and, indeed, in a way established a pattern for this all-American ballet company. However, one of the English choreographers, Andrée Howard, did not enjoy great success. She staged Death and the Maiden and Lady Into Fox, but these two productions were instantly dropped from the repertory.

Another of the British choreographic recruits, who was to become one of the vital forces of Ballet Theatre, was Antony Tudor. Tudor had been trained by Marie Rambert at her ballet club in London, and had really only come to America because Frederick Ashton, Pleasant's original choice for the British choreographer, had turned the job down. Tudor arrived with his principal male dancer, Hugh Laing, and together they changed the face of American ballet. During that first season Tudor staged Jardin aux Lilas, The Judgment of Paris, and Dark Elegies. Revivals from Marie Rambert's Ballet Club in London, they are still part of ABT's repertory.

Ballet Theatre started to tour and enjoyed the same success across the country that it had experienced in New York. However, Pleasant found himself in deeper and deeper trouble with the sponsors, who simply could not provide him with the amount of money his aspirations demanded. Nevertheless, he went on planning. He initiated a new Tudor ballet set to Schönberg's Verklärte Nacht; this, of course, was to become Pillar of Fire. Other of Pleasant's schemes were abandoned, including a new work that was to be choreographed by Doris Humphrey; it would have been the first collaboration of American classic ballet and American modern dance.

Pleasant moved on, but the company continued. For a time it was managed by that redoubtable American impresario, Sol Hurok, who changed its direction. He had it billed as "the greatest in Russian ballet," which for an American company must have been a litttle discouraging. However, the company continued to develop, new dancers joined, and the repertory was expanded. Among the dancers who added significantly to the company's reputation during this period were Alicia Markova, the first great British classic ballerina, whose initial stint with the company lasted from 1941 to 1946; Irina Baronova, who danced with the company between 1941 and 1943; and André Eglevsky, who was with the company in 1942 and 1943. This was a time of growth.

My first experience with American Ballet Theatre came on July 4, 1946, when the company made its first overseas tour. It was appearing at the Royal Opera House, Covent Garden, London, and it played there for at least eight weeks. It was an interesting year for the ballet in Britain. Since 1939 Britain had been isolated by the war. No visiting companies came until the opening of Boris Kochno's Les Ballets des Champs-Elysées on April 9, 1946. On June 17 Serge Lifar opened with his postwar company, Le Nouveau Ballet de Monte Carlo, starring Yvette Chauviré, and on July 4 Ballet Theatre made its London debut with Les Sylphides, Jerome Robbins's Fancy Free, and Michel Fokine's Bluebeard. The company was led by Lucia Chase, Nora Kaye, Alicia Alonso, Diana Adams, Melissa Hayden, André Eglevsky, Hugh Laing, John Kriza, Dimitri Romanoff, Jerome Robbins, and Michael Kidd. O brave new world that had such dancers in it.

At this point American Ballet Theatre had reached the first of its peaks. Its repertory was remarkably interesting. Yes, it was dominated by Tudor; not only did it give revivals of Tudor ballets already seen in London—Gala Performance and Jardin aux Lilas—but there were also three new major Tudor pieces: Pillar of Fire, Romeo and Juliet, and Undertow. There was also a new Americana repertory created by Jerome Robbins, Agnes de Mille, and Michael Kidd. The company was simply a revelation. It provided something quite different from the more staid approach of Britain's own Sadler's Wells Ballet, which was, of course, to become in time the Royal Ballet.

Yet, it seemed that something of that same staid approach was wanted by Ballet Theatre. That year, immediately following the company's London triumph, the then executive manager of Ballet Theatre, Peter Lawrence, issued to Ballet Annual in Britain what was called A Statement of Policy. It started by saying that "the directors of this young company . . .

hope to establish a permanent institution for the furthering of the ballet arts in America. It is a complicated task." The statement continued with a mention of the success of its nationwide tour but pointed out:

It is the commercial, or financial, necessity of these successful trans-continental tours that has caused Ballet Theatre to remain a "temporary" business venture hinged solely to the whims of theatrical entrepreneurs and booking managements.

This is not the goal of the directors of Ballet Theatre. Realizing that any assistance from the government of the United States as an important part of cultural life in the nation is at least a decade off, the management is striving to establish a permanent fund for the continued artistic production of ballet that will allow for the establishing of many vital assets without which a true repertory company cannot long exist. These include a permanent home, a Ballet Theatre school and funds with which to produce new works with proper rehearsal and offer better security and artistic program to its artists.

It is interesting that the problems of Ballet Theatre in 1946 are not all that dissimilar to the problems of Ballet Theatre in 1976. Over the years, Ballet Theatre has experienced more ups and downs than a clown on a trampoline. In part, this can be attributed to its lack of a permanent base; it has experimented inconclusively with Washington, and it has flirted continuously with New York, but somehow that elusive home has never come its way.

The story of the last thirty years is extraordinarily mixed. One of Ballet Theatre's major difficulties has been the absence of a major choreographer as a continuing presence. New York City Ballet has always been blessed with George Balanchine. Up until comparatively few years ago the Royal Ballet enjoyed the services of Frederick Ashton. At the beginning Ballet Theatre was extraordinarily fortunate in having Antony Tudor, but from about the middle 1940s on, Tudor has not been particularly productive. While his earlier ballets have always been a mainstay of the Ballet Theatre repertory, until quite recently he has not really been a creative force, but rather a creative inspiration. He has undoubtedly influenced several American choreographers, including Jerome

Robbins, but Robbins's stay with the company was fairly brief. As a result the company's ballets—a surprising number of which were borrowed in the first place from other companies' repertories—largely consist of pre-World War II classics of some kind or another: the Tudor repertory; what might be called De Mille and Robbins Americana repertory; and a floating number of novelties, few of which seem to remain in the permanent repertory, although once in a while a production such as the company's revival of Harald Lander's *Etudes* finds a permanent niche.

Yes, it is an eclectic repertory.

Many other choreographers have contributed to Ballet Theatre, notably Agnes de Mille, who has provided a whole library of works in a distinctively American tradition. Other choreographers have included Glen Tetley, John Neumeier, Michael Smuin, Dennis Nahat, Herbert Ross, Alvin Ailey, and notably, if perhaps all too briefly, Eliot Feld, who seemed to be the best hope for a Ballet Theatre resident choreographer since the days of Jerome Robbins.

A company is as good as its dancers, and its dancers are as good as its choreographers permit. Ballet Theatre has always maintained a very high standard of dancer. Possessing an extraordinarily eclectic repertory, it has also been instrumental in reviving many ballets from Europe. The company has passed through very dismal periods, but even during these periods the dancers it was offering were among the finest in the world. For example, during the first twenty years of its existence, up until 1960, Ballet Theatre featured Diana Adams, Alicia Alonso, Sonia Arova, Jean Babilée, Irina Baronova, Todd Bolender, Erik Bruhn, Karen Conrad, Leon Danielian, Anton Dolin, Scott Douglas, André Eglevsky, Royes Fernandez, Paul Godkin, Nana Gollner, Melissa Hayden, Rosella Hightower, Nora Kaye, Ruth Ann Koesun, John Kriza, Hugh Laing, Harold Lang, David Lichine, Michael Lland, Alicia Markova, Leonide Massine, Michael Maule, James Mitchell, Mary Ellen Moylan, Nicolas Orloff, Sono Osato, Tatiana Riabouchinska, Jerome Robbins, Dimitri Romanoff, Lupe Serrano, Maria Tallchief, Marjorie Tallchief, Tamara Toumanova, Antony Tudor, Violette Verdy, Sallie Wilson, and Igor Youskevitch.

Toward the end of the fifties and into the early sixties, ABT appeared to be in rather poor artistic shape. At times, it seemed amazing that the company continued. Slowly it pulled itself around. For example, the company's first revival of *Etudes* by the Danish choreographer Harald Lander was by all people's account a vital performance. The first Ballet Theatre production was at the Fifty-fourth Street Theater, New York, on October 5, 1961, with a cast headed by Toni Lander, Royes Fernandez, and Bruce Marks. Yet, the company was still not in exceptional shape. Its twenty-fifth anniversary season produced comparatively little of importance, but in the spring of 1965 the company played its first season at Lincoln Center in the then almost brand-new New York State Theater. On March 30, 1965, Jerome Robbins staged his new ballet to the score of Stravinsky's *Les Noces*. Nijinska had choreographed the original version, but Robbins had not seen this, and he produced a totally new, entirely envigorating recension of the work. It was a knockout and it opened the door to a new world for Ballet Theatre.

At this time, 1965—which, to make a personal note, was the time I emigrated from Britain to become the dance critic of the *New York Times*—Ballet Theatre was still very much in the shadow of the New York City Ballet and was also being threatened by the fresh vitality of a comparative newcomer to the scene, the Joffrey Ballet, which was just about to become a permanent constituent of the New York dance mix.

The company continued to experience problems about where it could appear. Sometimes it would be the New York State Theater, occasionally it would risk the Metropolitan Opera House, and then it would give a season at the Brooklyn Academy of Music. Its tours outside of New York were scattered and spasmodic. And, all in all, its artistic direction seemed scattered, without any particular focus. The company still had a major repertory and it still had some of the most interesting dancers as well. A company that could display Carla Fracci and Erik Bruhn in *Les Sylphides* or Lupe Serrano and Royes Fernandez in *Swan Lake* could not be all bad.

The aforementioned *Swan Lake* is indicative of a new trend in American Ballet Theatre's direction at this time. Lucia Chase and her long-time co-artistic director Oliver Smith, who have guided the company virtually ever since Richard Pleasant's resignation in 1941, first saw the Sadler's Wells (Royal) Ballet's production of *The Sleeping Beauty* in 1946, and it became their ambition to preserve Russian classics for the American public in the same manner as the Sadler's Wells (Royal Ballet) was preserving them. Economics were a perilous factor in this ambition. In the first place, a full-evening ballet was enormously expensive to stage, and in the second, there was no indication that the American public was ready to accept works of this length. The American dance audience had been nurtured on the principle of the triple bill, and it seemed at the beginning as though one work lasting an entire evening might be more than America could take. Oddly enough, it was the first visit of the Sadler's Wells Ballet (now the Royal Ballet) to the Metropolitan Opera House in 1949 that turned the tide. The company's productions of full-evening works, such as *The Sleeping Beauty*, *Swan Lake*, and *Cinderella*, none of which had been seen before in their entirety in America, created an appetite for the full-evening ballet that was later whetted by performances from companies such as the Bolshoi Ballet from Moscow, the Kirov Ballet from Leningrad, and the Royal Danish Ballet from Copenhagen. Suddenly, American Ballet Theatre found itself in a situation where it really had to present the old nineteenth-century Russian classics.

However, this was in no way a contradiction of its original artistic policy. It had always proclaimed its intention to preserve the best of the old, always maintaining its stance as an international museum of dance. Just as the art world insists on the existence of a Museum of Modern Art, it also must have a Metropolitan Museum of Art. The past has its needs and glories as does the future. It therefore became almost an imperative necessity that Ballet Theatre move into the realm of full-evening Russian classics.

As far as the classics were concerned, Ballet Theatre already had a *Giselle* that had probably outworn its usefulness, a *La Fille Mal Gardée* in a very whimsical version, and, of course, a number of the Fokine works, with their choreography decently reconstructed but generally poorly staged. For some years, Lucia Chase and Oliver Smith had dreamed of presenting either *The Sleeping Beauty* or *Swan Lake*; in fact, as early as 1946 wishes were expressed that *The Sleeping Beauty* might be staged, but nothing came of those aspirations. Aside from the difficulty of accustoming an audience to a full-length classic, touring conditions were still primitive, and the size of the company was considerably smaller then. In 1946 the company numbered only thirty-five dancers; as of 1976 it includes eighty-one guest artists. Moreover, the idea of playing one-, two-, or three-night stands in a vast range of cities had become impracticable; the company, which was playing in-

creasingly more in New York, by now was only appearing in the larger cities and staying for periods of up to three weeks.

Once one has decided to produce the two Tchaikovsky classics, it remains to be decided which version one is to choose. Since the Sadler's Wells (now the Royal) Ballet in London first produced its full-length *Swan Lake* in 1934 and followed it with a full-length *Sleeping Beauty* in 1939, these two ballets have become classic mainstays for the British repertory. Considerable care was taken to reproduce as nearly as possible the original 1895 *Swan Lake* choreography by Marius Petipa and Lev Ivanov and the original 1890 Petipa choreography for *The Sleeping Beauty*, both of which were first presented in St. Petersburg. These productions had been supervised and realized by Petipa's assistant at Maryinsky Theatre in St. Petersburg, Nicolai Sergeyev. Every attempt was made to make these productions choreographically similar to the original.

Since those two epoch-making British revivals, both ballets have entered the international repertories. Today, almost every major company has at least one and probably both of these works in its repertory, but usually in choregraphy that is a far cry from the Russian original, and this is, of course, today also true in Soviet Russia itself.

Lucia Chase and Oliver Smith made the strict, but in the end surprisingly daring, decision to maintain the original Petipa and Ivanov versions. Sergeyev himself was long dead, and although there were possibly people in Russia, such as Feodor Lopokhov, who might have some memories of the original, it would have been impossible to bring them to the West, so the only alternative was to explore British sources. As a result, the decision was made to ask the English ballet master David Blair to mount a full-length *Swan Lake*. It premiered at the Civic Opera House in Chicago on February 16, 1967, with the British ballerina Nadia Nerina as Odette and Royes Fernandez as Prince Siegfried. *The Sleeping Beauty* proved more difficult to incorporate into the repertory. Just as the company, almost from its beginning, had included the second act of *Swan Lake* in its repertory, so did it also present, on a far more intermittent basis, the last act of *The Sleeping Beauty* in a production called *Aurora's Wedding*. In the summer of 1974 the company staged the last act of *The Sleeping Beauty* in a version by David Blair following the original, as a beginning to its production of the complete ballet. This did not prove particularly successful, and so for the complete ballet the decision was made to reproduce as far as possible, even including the original scenery and costumes by Oliver Messel, the version that the Sadler's Wells (now the Royal) Ballet first produced in London in 1946.

In between the productions of *Swan Lake* and *The Sleeping Beauty* the company produced or refurbished many of its other classic productions. David Blair's production of *Giselle* entered the repertory on July 10, 1968, while Erik Bruhn's new staging of *La Sylphide* came on July 13, 1972. The reproduction of the classic Russian repertory went on rapidly. On July 3, 1974, Natalia Makarova staged "The Kingdom of the Shades" scene from Petipa's *La Bayadère*. Another full-evening Petipa ballet was introduced on June 26, 1975, when Rudolf Nureyev staged *Raymonda* for the company. For a couple of the ballets it was decided that authenticity could not be hoped for, so the company chose to produce contemporary versions instead. *La Fille Mal Gardée* was newly staged by Dimitri Romanoff on January 13, 1972, though it did include much of the traditional Russian version, particularly in its mime sequences. However, the earlier production of *Coppélia* by Enrique Martinez, first seen on December 24, 1968, was virtually a new ballet, although it of course adhered strictly to the original 1870 version of the story.

It must be admitted that sometimes additions to the repertory have seemed whimsical and also not infrequently opportunistic. In a way this is a dancer's company rather than a choreographer's company, which explains Lucia Chase's loyalty to her dancers and also the fact that the company's audiences are always more interested in *who* is dancing than what is being danced.

The artistic direction of the company has varied a great deal since its founding by Richard Pleasant. This function was at first assumed by Lucia Chase, who for a long time has served as the artistic power behind the company; however, her codirector Oliver Smith has played an integral role in company policy and planning since 1945. Other people also have been concerned with the artistic direction of the company. For two years immediately prior to the company's European debut in London in 1946, Antony Tudor was named artistic administrator. Briefly, following that period, there was an artistic committee consisting of Lucia Chase, Henry Clifford, Aaron Copland, Agnes de Mille, Jerome Robbins, Oliver Smith, and Antony Tudor. And for the past three years Antony Tudor has served as the company's associate director and has a great deal to do with the day-to-day operation of the troupe.

Another element in the company's direction has been the power of the two past presidents of the Ballet Theatre Foundation, which today represents the company. Sherwin M. Goldman, president of the Ballet Theatre Foundation from 1969 to 1974, did a great deal to strengthen the company's board of directors and to reorganize its structure and functions. These very important years for Ballet Theatre were also internally abrasive because of the strained relationship between Chase and Goldman, who often seem to lock in some kind of power struggle. However, the company emerged at the end of Goldman's presidency in an infinitely healthier condition than it had been in at the beginning.

Goldman's successor, Justin S. Colin, is not, as was Goldman, also the company's chief executive; yet, he too carries far more weight in the councils of the company than did presidents of the foundation in the pre-Goldman era. Also, the company today can boast a strong stage and classroom team in its assistant director, Enrique Martinez; regisseur, Dimitri Romanoff; and its ballet masters, Michael Lland, Scott Douglas, and until her death in 1976, Fiorella Keane.

Today, one of the most crucial artistic issues facing the company is the subject of guest stars. Ballet Theatre has always existed as a kind of repository of a wide variety of ballets, and over the past few seasons it has also become a repository of international ballet guest stars. During the past season, for example, among the dancers who made guest appearances in New York were Mikhail Baryshnikov, Erik Bruhn, Richard Cragun, Hideo Fukagawa, Marcia Haydée, Natalia Makarova, Yoko Morishita, Rudolf Nureyev, and Lynn Seymour. Some of these dancers have been more closely connected with the company than have others; these include Baryshnikov, Makarova, and especially Bruhn, whose association with Ballet Theatre goes back to 1949. The guest stars certainly helped to make Ballet Theatre's nine-week 1976 summer season—and its earlier winter season at the Uris Theatre—one of its most exciting. The itinerant ballet super-star has become a new factor in ballet life, just as the super-star has been a reality in opera ever since the advent of jet travel. Some of the resident dancers in Ballet Theatre have vigorously objected to this growing development and increasing dependence upon guest artists. However, it is safe to say that this custom is here to stay, and it certainly does add to the texture and substance of a ballet theatre company.

The question hanging over American Ballet Theatre as it ends its thirty-sixth season is probably that of directorial succession. The force behind Ballet Theatre all these years has clearly been Lucia Chase, and I have been given to understand that Miss Chase intends to retire in about two years' time. Lucia Chase has not merely been the most generous patron in the history of American ballet; she has always been a woman not at all reluctant to put her mouth where her money was, and has ruled the company with a whim of iron. Her dancers have always enjoyed a great personal connection with her; many of them have become personal friends; and she runs the entire company rather as if she were a mixture of stern matriarch and village lady bountiful. She keeps casting very much within her control and also maintains a fairly firm hand over the repertory. People who have worked with her say she will often listen to reason, but often will not.

Lucia Chase does not seem to have groomed anyone to be her successor, but the logical choice would seem to fall on her loyal codirector, Oliver Smith. But other choices may be made. In the next two years, Rudolf Nureyev might feel like hanging up his ballet slippers, or at least giving them more of a rest than they enjoy at present, and taking over the direction of a company. American Ballet Theatre might be a very interesting company for him to take over. Neither is it inconceivable that Robert Joffrey could be persuaded to combine his own Joffrey Ballet with Ballet Theatre, giving the new company both a large and a small group, rather along the lines of Britain's Royal Ballet.

The other not inconsiderable aspect is the dis-

covery of a permanent home, presumably in New York, for the wandering Ballet Theatre. In 1977 the company is risking its longest season ever at the Metropolitan Opera House. Perhaps this will lead to a closer relationship in the future, since the Metropolitan Opera House is the only major opera house of international status still playing a long season and attempting to give seven performances a week. In every other house the prohibitive cost of opera has resulted in a reduction in the number of performances, usually to three or four a week, with the ballet company (which is far cheaper to run) assuming responsibility for the other performances. It is no secret that Anthony A. Bliss, head of the Metropolitan Opera, has been exploring the possibility of bringing full-time ballet into the house, which would involve either forming a new company, based perhaps on the present Opera Ballet, or importing a company from outside, which could be Ballet Theatre, or just possibly New York City Ballet, or an expanded version of the Joffrey Ballet, of which by chance Bliss happens to be chairman of the Board.

While the future is not precisely clear for American Ballet Theatre, its past, even with all its vicissitudes, has been remarkably distinguished. If the inspiration for the company belonged to Richard Pleasant, and that extraordinary idea was his, it was Lucia Chase who from the beginning encouraged him and Chase who, together with her codirector, Oliver Smith, and her artistic mentor, Antony Tudor, pushed the idea of Ballet Theatre to success. It is very rare that people can live to see the ripened fruits of their efforts to nurture a great artistic institution from seed, particularly in a country like our own that has no real tradition of institutions in the performing arts. And yet, this is precisely what Chase has accomplished. Ballet Theatre, with its lengthy overseas tours and its hospitality to dancers from all over the world, has become a major force, not just in American ballet but in the entire world of international dance.

New
Productions

Opposite and on following page, Natalia Makarova in Jerome Robbin's *Other Dances*. © 1976; from *Waldman on Dance*, William Morrow & Co., 1977, by permission.

Mikhail Baryshnikov in Twyla Tharp's *Push Comes to Shove*.

Martine van Hamel and Clark Tippet in Kenneth MacMillan's *Solitaire*.

LOUIS PÉRES

Hilda Morales, Richard Schafer, Michael Owen, Amy Blaisdell, Marianna Tcher-kassky, and Charles Ward in Antony Tudor's *The Leaves Are Fading*.

BEVERLEY GALLEGOS

Martine van Hamel, Clark Tippet, Charles Ward, and Cynthia Gregory in Glen Tetley's *Gemini*.

At *left*, Clark Tippet and Martine van Hamel in Glen Tetley's *Le Sacre du Printemps*.

On the following pages, Mikhail Baryshnikov and Natalia Makarova in Glen Tetley's *Le Sacre du Printemps*.

19

BEVERLEY GALLEGOS

BEVERLEY GALLEGOS

Mikhail Baryshnikov and Judith Jamison in Alvin Ailey's *Pas de Duke*.

Mikhail Baryshnikov in Glen Tetley's *Le Sacre du Printemps*.

LOUIS PÉRES

Mikhail Baryshnikov and Bonnie Mathis in Roland Petit's *Le Jeune Homme et la Mort*.

24

LOUIS PÉRES

25

Erik Bruhn and Natalia Makarova in John Neumeier's *Epilogue*.

On the following page, Natalia Makarova in John Neumeier's *Epilogue*.

JACK MITCHELL

Heritage

Mikhail Mordkin rehearsing Patricia Bowman, Lucia Chase, and Karen Conrad
in the Ballet Theatre production of Mordkin's *Voices of Spring*, 1940.

PROMINENT
JUNIOR LEAGUE
PUPIL

To Mr. Mordkin

*with the greatest appreciation
of the privilege of studying
with him*

LUCIA CHASE

Lucia's ad in Mordkin program.
Courtesy of Michael Mordkin, Jr.

Portrait of Mikhail Mordkin. Courtesy of Michael Mordkin, Jr.

Annabelle Lyon as The Lustful One, Agnes de Mille as The Fanatical One, and Lucia Chase as The Greedy One in De Mille's *Three Virgins and a Devil*, 1941.

CARL VAN VECHTEN

Hugh Laing and Nora Kaye in Tudor's *Pillar of Fire*, 1942.

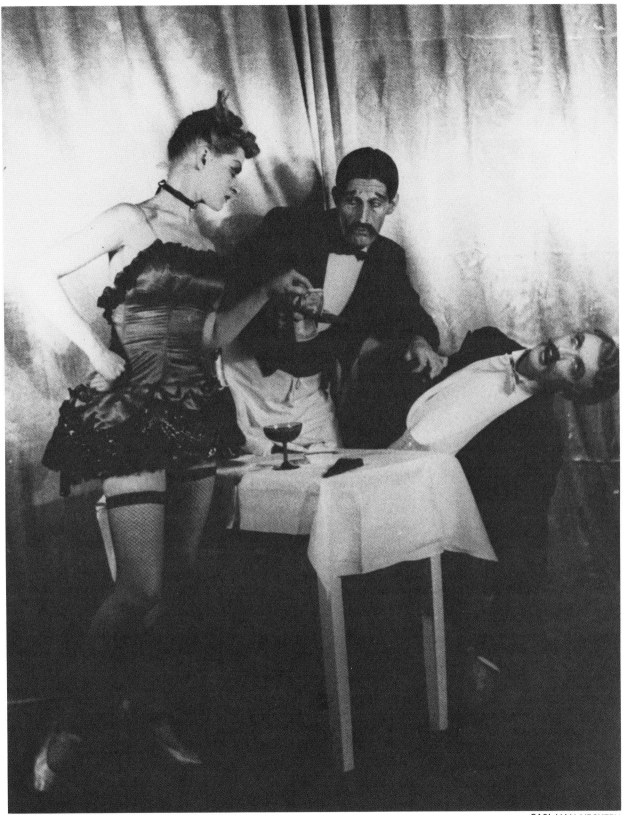

Maria Karnilova, Hugh Laing, and Antony Tudor in Tudor's *The Judgment of Paris*, 1943.

Hugh Laing, Nora Kaye, and Antony Tudor in Tudor's *Dark Elegies*, 1943.

Hugh Laing and Nana Gollner in Tudor's *Shadow of the Wind*, 1948.

ALFREDO VALENTE

WALTER E. OWEN

Opposite, Alicia Markova and Anton Dolin in *Giselle*. *Above*, Alicia Alonso in act 2 of *Giselle*. On the following pages, Alicia Markova and Igor Youskevitch in Balanchine's *Theme and Variations* and Alicia Alonso and Fernando Alonso in Tudor's *Undertow*.

ALFREDO VALENTE

WALTER E. OWEN

Jerome Robbins in his own *Fancy Free*.

Above, Gayle Young. *Below,* Bruce Marks in *Helen of Troy.*

JACK MITCHELL

43

JACK MITCHELL

JACK MITCHELL

Maria Tallchief as Odette in *Swan Lake*.

Toni Lander as Odette in *Swan Lake*.

Royes Fernandez as Prince Siegfried in *Swan Lake*.   JACK MITCHELL

At *left*, Erik Bruhn as Albrecht in *Giselle*.

On the following page, Erik Bruhn and Nora Kaye in the *pas de deux* from *Paquita*.

Classic Repertory

Natalia Makarova and Fernando Bujones in *La Bayadère*.

BEVERLEY GALLEGOS

Mikhail Baryshnikov as Franz in *Coppélia*.

At *left*, Gelsey Kirkland and Mikhail Baryshnikov in *Coppélia*.

Mikhail Baryshnikov in *Coppélia*.

Eleanor D'Antuono and Fernando Bujones in *Coppélia*.

Mikhail Baryshnikov and Gelsey Kirkland in the *pas de deux* from *Le Corsaire*.

Zhandra Rodriquez and John Prinz in the *pas de deux* from *Le Corsaire*.

Eleanor D'Antuono in the *pas de deux* from *Don Quixote*.

DINA MAKAROVA

Mikhail Baryshnikov in the *pas de deux* from *Don Quixote*.

Niels Kehlet and Carla Fracci in *La Fille Mal Gardée*.

Yoko Morishita and Fernando Bujones in the *pas de deux* from *Don Quixote*.

DINA MAKAROVA

Mikhail Baryshnikov in *La Fille Mal Gardée*.

Mikhail Baryshnikov and Natalia Makarova in *La Fille Mal Gardée*.

Carla Fracci and Erik Bruhn in *Giselle*.

Erik Bruhn, Richard Gain, and Carla Fracci in *Giselle*.

LOUIS PÉRES

Eleanor D'Antuono and Ted Kivitt in *Giselle*.

Carla Fracci and Erik Bruhn in *Giselle*.

Marcos Paredes, Eleanor D'Antuono, and Dennis Nahat in *Petrouchka.*

Dennis Nahat and Erik Bruhn in *Petrouchka*.

BEVERLEY GALLEGOS

Erik Bruhn as The Saracen in Nureyev's *Raymonda*.

At *left*, *Petrouchka* with Sallie Wilson as The Nursemaid and Rudolf Nureyev
as Jean de Brienne in Nureyev's staging of *Raymonda*.

Gelsey Kirkland and Ivan Nagy in the 1976 Oliver Messel production of *The Sleeping Beauty*.

Natalia Makarova and Charles Ward in act 1 "Rose Adagio" of *The Sleeping Beauty.*   DINA MAKAROVA

71

Natalia Makarova in *Swan Lake*.

Cynthia Gregory as Odile in *Swan Lake*.

Ivan Nagy in act 1 of *La Sylphide*.

Toni Lander and Royes Fernandez, *center,* in *La Sylphide.*

Carla Fracci and Erik Bruhn in *La Sylphide*.

At *left*, Cynthia Gregory and Michael Denard in *La Sylphide*.

On the following pages, Gelsey Kirkland and Mikhail Baryshnikov in *La Sylphide*. And Natalia Makarova and Ivan Nagy in *La Sylphide*.

BEVERLEY GALLEGOS

Ruth Ann Koesun in *Les Sylphides*.

JACK MITCHELL

Les Sylphides with Eleanor D'Antuono, Ivan Nagy, Christine Sarry, and Karena Brock.

BIL LEIDERSDORF

The
Choreographers

Antony Tudor

Anyone seeing Antony Tudor in 1925 working as an errand boy in London's Smithfield Meat Market would hardly have predicted that he would one day become one of the world's foremost choreographers, yet only six years later he was making his first creative attempts—and successful ones, at that—with the Ballet Rambert. He was originally inspired to enter the dance world by his contact with the performances of the Pavlova and Diaghilev companies and by the thought of the extensive travel such a career would afford. But once with Rambert, he recognized that he did not have the technique to become a great dancer and he therefore opted for choreography. It is to Marie Rambert's eternal credit that she helped foster Tudor's budding talent, and it is partly owing to the stimulating and creative atmosphere surrounding her Ballet Club in the small, even miniscule Mercury Theatre that he was able, in the late thirties, to turn out three major works in rapid succession. These were *Jardin aux Lilas* (1936), *Dark Elegies* (1937), and *The Judgment of Paris* (1938).

In 1938 Tudor left Rambert to form his own London Ballet, for which he created *Gala Performance*. The following year he was invited by director Richard Pleasant to join Ballet Theatre.

CB: When did you first hear of Ballet Theatre and how did you become involved with it?

AT: Fred Ashton had been asked to come and do some ballet participation in the opening season for Ballet Theatre. He had to refuse because of prior commitments, plus, I believe, because he didn't like to fly and had not been too happy with the American scene while working on the Gertrude Stein/Virgil Thomson opera *Four Saints in Three Acts*. Whereupon Agnes de Mille, who was working quite closely with Richard Pleasant, told him about this young genius, and Mr. Pleasant then contracted both this young genius and Hugh Laing, who at that time was working with Miss de Mille as her partner in her recitals. Said young genius and Hugh Laing signed their contracts in the summer of 1939, and the rest is HISTORY!

CB: What is your most vivid recollection of the early years?

AT: Arriving on Columbus Day when the banks were closed, and, bonds not having been posted, having to spend the night at Ellis Island. And being surprised at what very good company we were in there. The lack of foresight implied by that bond stiuation hinted at the shape of things to come.

Thus, on the recommendation of Agnes de Mille, who had known him from her own English days, Antony Tudor was invited to join the Ballet Theatre company. Except for the season 1945–46, Tudor remained with the company steadily until 1950. For them he staged many of his English works and went on to choreograph, among others, *Pillar of Fire* (1942), *Romeo and Juliet* and *Dim Lustre* (1943), *Undertow* (1945), *Shadow of the Wind* (1948), and *Nimbus* (1950). There followed a twenty-five-year stretch during which he choreographed a few minor works which were presented at Jacob's Pillow; *La Gloire* (1952) for New York City Ballet; an important work about war for the Royal Swedish Ballet, *Echoing of Trumpets* (1963); and two major works for the Royal Ballet, *Shadowplay* (1967) and a comedy, *Knight Errant* (1968). But his formal association with ABT had been dissolved, and he was, for the most part, concentrating on teaching. Had he never produced another work, his legacy would have carried sufficient weight to win him a significant place in ballet history, but fortunately, in 1975 he made a choreographic comeback. The result was *The Leaves Are Fading*. It proved an inventive and hauntingly lovely piece.

Since his early days Tudor has passed through several emotional psychological phases, which probably have been reflected in his work. In the opening years of the forties, he became engrossed in Freudian psychiatry (though by his own admission his personal encounters with analysis were fleeting and abortive), and his ballets from those years tended to focus on the psychology of human relationships. For *Undertow* alone, a ballet built around the disturbance of a youth rejected from infancy, he absorbed thirty-four books on psychiatry. His earlier works, *Lilac Garden* and *Pillar of Fire* reflect something of the same preoccupation. Tudor's unique viewpoint was expressed not only in his choice of story line but also in his assigning of roles, for which he preferred the interesting dancer to the classically perfect one, and in his use of the total body rather than conventional mime as a means of expression. Consider how in one of the private moments of *Lilac Garden* the discarded woman ("An Episode in His Past") faces her lover across the stage and suddenly rushes at him, leaping onto his shoulder. He grasps her tightly without bothering to look up; he doesn't need to. Tudor has built the couple's silent, desperate communication into the pose. As Agnes de Mille has

expressed it: "With Tudor every movement has a meaning; an arabesque can be a sigh." This does not imply that Tudor gives his dancers explicit direction. Sallie Wilson, foremost among the present generation of Tudor exponents, recalls that when she learned *Dark Elegies* under his guidance at Jacob's Pillow, she was taught the steps of the dance but not the mood he envisioned that the character was to project. Tudor's apparent oversight is no accident. By keeping the dancers guessing, he keeps them literally on their toes—constantly seeking new means of establishing the dramatic impact of their roles.

Perhaps because he once assimilated so much psychoanalytic literature, Tudor now functions very much like an analyst himself. He does not specifically tell his dancers what to do, but he suggests a course of action that they can develop on their own. He has also been known to dispense brutal criticism sometimes to test his opponent's strength, sometimes to spur on renewed efforts, and sometimes to start the person thinking along apparently independent lines, which are actually those of Tudor's own making. Despite this disconcerting feature, all the artists who have worked with Tudor have ultimately recognized that the wounds they have sustained were inflicted on them for their own good, and that collaborating with him is never less than a thrilling experience.

For his part, Tudor has been fortunate in having had on more than one occasion the ideal clay at his disposal. In his most productive years he found perfect interpreters in Nora Kaye and Hugh Laing. More recently Sallie Wilson, Carla Fracci, Natalia Makarova, Lynn Seymour, and Marcia Haydée have performed his ballets with some success.

For many years Tudor served as director of the Metropolitan Opera Ballet School, and assisted on the faculty of the Juilliard School of Music, Dance Department. His choreographic imagination was never entirely at rest, however, for even during this period he was choreographing small works at Jacob's Pillow and arranging simple pieces for the annual graduation performances of his Juilliard students. It was at Juilliard that he began experiments with the steps that were eventually to lead to *The Leaves Are Fading*. Tudor is so unpredictable in his rate of output, if not in his quality of inspiration, that it is impossible to say whether or not future seasons at ABT will include new offerings from him. His past success may be a mixed blessing, for he knows that the ballets he has already created are works of such enduring validity that his reputation could survive on them alone.

The Tudor phenomenon is aptly summed up by his most important early collaborators. Hugh Laing puts it: "Tudor sometimes seems hard . . . but he has respect for his performers. You are not his tool; his string-pulling lets you be alive on stage."* Nora Kaye has stated: "[When] he put me in *Dark Elegies* . . . that changed my life as a dancer, and as a person. Suddenly dance had a new focus for me. He is the only choreographer I know who really has genius."* But Tudor himself knows better than anyone where he as a person stands in relation to his work: "I am the most cold-blooded son-of-a-bitch that ever happened, but my characters aren't.**

Agnes de Mille

This interview with Agnes de Mille took place in her apartment in New York City during the summer of 1976. De Mille's life and times have been beautifully documented by De Mille herself in a series of autobiographical books. She is one of the finest writers on dance this or any other century has produced.

Like Tudor and Robbins her relationship with Ballet Theatre has been long established and ongoing. Yet she has not been so central to Ballet Theatre's repertory as Tudor—she would be the first to admit that—and she never made quite the stir that Robbins made, first with *Fancy Free* and then, many years later, with *Les Noces*. Indeed, De Mille's best-known work for Ballet Theatre, *Rodeo*, was originally created for Serge Denham's Ballet Russe de Monte Carlo.

However, I have quoted Agnes at length for several reasons. Partly because I discovered in talking to her that I loved her—I have reservations about her work, but she has many reservations about mine—because she was willing to talk freely and frankly about the beginnings of Ballet Theatre, and because she has a memory like a computer bank.

Of my three Ballet Theatre choreographers, I realize that Agnes is taking the lioness's share of the

* Selma Jeanne Cohen, "Antony Tudor: The Years in America and After," *Dance Perspectives* 18 (1963): p. 79; p. 76.

** John Gruen, *The Private World of Ballet* (New York: Viking Press, (1975), p. 267.

JACK MITCHELL

space. But while Tudor and Jerry (both of whom I obviously admire enormously) might have talked as long, they would never have had the courage to have talked so well. Agnes is liberated. And she says just and precisely what is on her heart. I like this interview. I think it is a document of the history of American Ballet Theatre.

CB: In 1939, you had virtually just come back from England. Did you ever choreograph anything for the Russian (Mordkin) Ballet?

ADM: Never. Nor had I seen them. I couldn't bear to go to ballet companies. I went to see the Ballet Russe de Monte Carlo, and on the whole I thought it was pretentious. I'm not a Massine fan at all. And during my stay in England, of course, he was absolute God at Covent Garden. Antony Tudor and I used to go to the very tip-top balcony—it was all we could afford—and we'd stand side by side quite silently, but that was an affront. The audience up there was screaming themselves hoarse, throwing up with excitement, and would turn on us with the most hostile expressions and dislike because we weren't carrying on like the rest of them. I disliked Massine, and his so-called symphonic ballets. I saw them in dress rehearsal. And I saw *Choreartium* on the stage at Covent Garden at midnight in practice clothes, black and white, all of them. Never looked so handsome in its life. Sacheverell Sitwell introduced Massine, saying "This is certainly the greatest choreographer we have living and probably ever have had," and I sank down in my seat and I thought of Graham. They'd never heard of her, they didn't want to hear—and I thought of various people. I thought of Antony Tudor out of Nottinghill Gate. He'd already done *Lilac Garden*. I came back to America, and Massine was still the god. . . .

CB: When did you come back here?

ADM: Well, the British Home Office got rid of me by refusing to let me have a permit for anything. It was late November 1938, right on the brink of war. We'd been through the false alarm. I had my gas mask, and eventually we came home. My mother was delighted to see me.

I had already met Richard Pleasant in 1936, dancing for the film of *Romeo and Juliet* with MGM. Just after I got back, Pleasant called me up and said, "I want you to come and see the Mordkin Ballet." I said, "I don't particularly want to see the Mordkin Ballet," and he said, "Well, they're nice tickets, Agnes, and they're free," and I said, "Well, that certainly is an inducement." He said, "René Blum is coming." I said, "You mean, you've got him to come?" and he said, "Oh, yes." I couldn't believe it. Well, I went, Blum was there, in fact Pleasant filled the house with the politesse.

CB: Now we're getting into 1939.

ADM: Nearly, not quite. But I was impressed by the audience. Patricia Bowman was the leading lady. I'd known her from way back at Roxy's. And Nina Stroganova—Nina Strom—she was lovely, and Miss Chase. So I went to the dressing room, fell all over Patty Bowman, was very flattering, was introduced to Nina, and was quite rude to Lucia, now that I look back on it, because I didn't say anything. The three leading ladies were sitting there, and I just didn't speak to Lucia.

Pleasant called me up a couple of months later. I think this was now June 1939. And he said "Come to lunch with Lucia Chase at the Italian Pavilion," and it also was free (and I was hungry). So I went there in a sassy hat, and Lucia was graciousness itself—she always is—and I sat down, and they were planning a company that would embrace everybody in the world. You'd just think of a name, and she'd say "Put it down on the list." And she said, "We've got to get a ballet choreographer—a new, young one. We're going to have Fokine, of course. But we think we'll get Freddy Ashton." And I said, "Don't get Freddy Ashton, I implore you. You get Antony Tudor." Lucia had never heard of him. So in explanation I said, "In the first place, Freddy's tied up with Sadler's Wells, heart and soul, and if you got him, it would only be for a very short time. And I don't think you'd get him. But if you got Tudor, he'd stay, probably, because I don't know how things are going. He has his own company now." He had it in Limehouse. But I didn't know how it was doing. Anyway, I said, "Just get him, but get him alone." They received no answer whatever. Did you know this?

CB: Yes, I knew something of this, a little.

ADM: Well, according to Peggy van Praagh and Terese Horner, both dancers in Tudor's company and my very good friends and dancers in my company, Tudor just hung on to the telegram. He didn't answer it. And then war was declared, and they were in it. Nobody could leave England. Well, he went to the local drafting office and produced the telegram, and it was predated, so they let him leave, and they let Hugh leave too because he was from Barbados and they couldn't keep him. Hugh paid his own way, and so did Andrée Howard. And the three came and Dolin, naturally. When Tudor arrived, he was a bit nervous about me, because he hadn't been very nice to me. In fact, he'd been terrible before I left, and we hadn't spoken for a long, long time. But I sent him cigarettes to the boat, and then I went to get him the night he arrived, and we all took him— Pleasant and I and others to Rockefeller Center—and he stood there stunned. Even Hugh was impressed. The speech was knocked out of him for once, then they got to work.

Pleasant asked me "What would you like to do?" and I said, "A Negro ballet." And the reason why I chose that was that I did not want to offer direct competition. I'd never done a ballet, never. So I said, "Give me my black girls, and I'll go into a room somewhere else, quietly." Well, that was a saga in itself, because it was very, very difficult. There were few black dancers at that time. And they were starving and they were disorderly. But I was separate and I fought my battles by myself. Anyhow, my ballet was pretty dreadful.

CB: This was *Black Ritual?*

ADM: Yes, yes. But it was a good piece of music —Milhaud. And, it had gorgeous decor, and also it was a serious effort. But it wasn't any good. It was a first effort, and I put everything I knew in it every two bars. Beginner's troubles. Meanwhile, Tudor was doing his works. During the first night of *Jardin aux Lilas* the audience was knocked senseless, particularly John Martin. And I said, "Wait till you see *Dark Elegies.*" Strangely enough *Dark Elegies* never caught on in the same way. I think it's equally beautiful. Absolutely astonishing. And, of course, I wanted to do *Dark Elegies* because I had created the fifth dance in London. Tudor never even suggested it. Lucia had the role. My dance. But, little by little, Tudor began to be friendly again. Then he asked me to do *The Judgment of Paris*, because no one else could do the Venus role.

CB: Had you done that for Ballet Rambert? You didn't do it?

ADM: I *commissioned* the ballet. It was created for me. Didn't you know that?

CB: No. Who did it?

ADM: I did it.

CB: You did it for Rambert?

ADM: No. Not for Rambert at all. I was doing a small series of dances as a curtain raiser to a Gogol play. The *Inspector General*, at that funny little theatre, the Westminster, right opposite the back door of Buckingham Palace. They asked me to do a series of my concert solos and comedies, but I needed something between them while I changed costumes. So I said get Hugh and Antony, and we'll have three of us and two girls, and I'll split the fee three ways, which is what we did. So, in effect, I commissioned it, and it was made for me. There were Terese Horner but—what did he call her? . . Terese Langfield. Charlotte Bidmead—he gave her a name and

it wasn't her name at all. Phyllis was her name. That was another point of irritation between us. He changed people's names. He put his thumbmark on every girl. I said, "You just let them have the name they were baptized with and that'll do." "No, no." So the girls were absolutely schizoid working for the two of us. The thing was that Antony wanted to grow, naturally, and was beginning to feel his strength, and it is an enormous talent, huge. I always said to him, "Antony, you have a far bigger talent than I. The papers write about me, but they don't know what they're writing about. It doesn't matter. I know it, and you know it, and everybody who has any sense knows it. Don't think of us as comparable." Rambert came to see the two of us in our little company, and she said, "You're both wonderful, but you just cancel each other out and this is a very bad combination." And she was absolutely right. But Tudor has never ever been able to let it alone. Ever. Now, that's too bad. He's too big. And there's no peace for him. He's done a great many things. A lot of them I didn't see, because he had said I'd stolen from him, which is just poppycock. And he knows it. But it was vicious, and so I just didn't see anything he'd done.

CB: What did you make of Richard Pleasant?

ADM: He was a lost soul.

CB: Really? How old was he. He must have been very young at this time. I mean, he died young.

ADM: Well, first of all, he was an alcoholic.

CB: From the beginning?

ADM: I didn't know it till later. But it was the end of his first year or his second year with Ballet Theatre that Lucia had to let him go. He wasn't responsible. He was curious and he was inventive and had a lot of ideas. He told me he wanted an entire literature of the dance world, and he was going to begin with eighteenth-century ballets and have them, and I said, "You can't possibly have them. I know a lot about them. They're gone. You can't have them, and if you had them, bringing Versailles and other bits of paraphernalia over, we'd be bored to death." The first year was a hodgepodge of all sorts of things, but they had a new opening night almost every night. There were people like Carl van Vechten, who came in the beginning and said, "My god, this is a miracle —this is like the early Diaghilev Ballet." Now, people forget that Diaghilev's Ballets Russes was a failure here. Absolute failure. And the houses were not full. And that Isadora Duncan was a failure as far as box office went. And that all her houses were empty and they were empty all across the continent. She never played to full houses. She played to head-lines but never to good houses. The entire Diaghilev company was stranded. Otto Kahn brought them home. There wasn't a taste for ballet. It began with Massine. He built it up, and Hurok. They did it.

CB: In 1933, with the baby ballerinas.

ADM: The first year it was a flop, too, although it was marvelous. But about 1936–1937 it began pack-ing them in, and by 1938 and 1939 it was marvelous box office. Ballet Theatre had a wonderful season, but it lost a great deal of money, of course.

CB: Lucia paid all the bills?

ADM: I guess she did. I don't know. Now, you'll have to ask her. She didn't take credit for anything. She hid. Lucia was a dancer, a ballerina, and she wanted to do all sorts of fancy dancing in tutus with Dolin, and that was the first really thorny opposition. She had terrible scenes with him. He'd say, "Oh, she's in a pet of anger, just infuriated, infuriated be-cause I wouldn't let her dance the lead." Well, she paid thousands, tens of thousands, and she couldn't see why she couldn't buy it. And he wouldn't give it to her. He danced with Patsy Bowman and then Nana Gollner.

CB: And Baronova.

ADM: Not yet. Nana came in the second year. Nana was supposed to be there the first year, but there was something wrong with her foot that year. So she came the second year. The second year we went to the Majestic, and on the opening night we did *Giselle* with Nana, I think, and then my *Three Virgins and a Devil*, which was a great success and I thought was stinking, and then Tudor's *Gala Per-formance*, which simply had them in the aisles. And Nana was the girl in black, the Italian. And John Martin said, "Well, of course, the man is an unques-tioned genius." All the critics said it was wonderful. No audience. Now, we had Alicia Alonso and Nora Kaye. Maria Karnilova, I think, was there from the beginning. But Nora came in the second year. That second year brought incredible people, including Jerry Robbins.

CB: But Kriza was there from the beginning?

ADM: I can't remember. You see, I never saw them. I didn't know them. And when I was in *Judg-ment*, I was only with Antony and Hugh. Lucia was

quite marvelous. And she was quite marvelous in *Virgins*, and I didn't think she was very good because she couldn't dance it, you see, as I wanted it danced, and I didn't think any of us were very funny. How can you tell when you're alone in a room dancing around what used to be Lawrence Langner's desk whether a thing is funny or not? You know? It didn't seem to me to be. And opening night there were ex-plosions of laughs, and I remember going backstage and saying, "Well, Lucia, you must have had the place packed with friends tonight!" I was really ob-noxious. When I consider my rudeness, I'm just astonished.

CB: Lucia is the sort of person who sometimes inspires rudeness because she's so gentle. Do you know what I mean? She has such politesse. There's always this element. Prim.

ADM: Prim, prissy.

CB: There's always this incredible amount that she knows better than anyone. And yet her innate good taste is not going to let her point this out. You know, it's one of those things—she ought to have been English.

ADM: Oh, no. This is New England.

CB: I suppose it is.

ADM: Oh, my dear, you don't know the New Eng-land character. Oh my, this is really the hard-shell Connecticut, what they call . . .

CB: The Connecticut Yankee.

ADM: Oh yes, oh yes.

CB: You left Ballet Theatre because . . .

ADM: I didn't leave. Lucia never signed me. I wanted with all my heart to be taken into the com-pany. And Antony would put me in ballet after ballet and call me for rehearsal, and Lucia would show up in my stead. And Antony was simply appalling to her in public, so I was told. I wasn't there because I wasn't called. And then Antony learned that he could abuse her. And he's just enough of a sadist to find fun in that, and she took, my God, what that woman took! Oh, she could buy and sell all of us, and she knew it, you see. But besides that, besides that was Lucia's deep feeling that there was some-thing worthwhile that she was going to get if she went through hell, and she went through hell.

CB: Incredible tenacity, that woman . . .

ADM: Well, Clive, I don't think, in the history of dancing—and you probably know as much as I—but I don't think there's been any other instance where one rich person decided they would have—what it amounted to was a toy. Because it wasn't her living. Therefore, it was a pleasure and it persisted long after she got what she wanted for her own vanity. But Chase has enormous character. And anyone who underestimates that is underestimating a national figure.

CB: How old is she?

ADM: I haven't the foggiest. I believe she is considerably older than I am, though it doesn't seem possible. That back is as straight . . . the legs are straight.

CB: She's extraordinary, isn't she?

ADM: And it's not an easy life she's had.

CB: No, I know. It's been a rough life. But she's always had this incredible resolution and this willingness to . . .

ADM: But she could adapt, you see, and that is the incredible thing. She couldn't be a ballerina, she couldn't be Giselle. But, you know, John Martin, who studied her very carefully, said that although she had no technique really, her idea of "The Prelude" in *Les Sylphides* is correct.

CB: I think in a way that's right. You know, she has an innate taste, which came out in dramatic roles.

ADM: Well, it's an interesting thing about Lucia . . . Another tragedy was that she wanted to do *Rodeo*. Oh, the pressure that was put on me was incredible. They didn't do *Rodeo* because Gerry Sevastianov was running Ballet Theatre at the time. He had no sense whatever, but he was running it, and he refused my scenario. The day after *Pillar of Fire* opened, I went to him and said, "I think this is one of the most astonishing things I've ever seen in the whole of my life." And he said, "Well, my dear, modern teachers may like it, but the general public *won't* like it. It will have no future. It won't even be a name in a year." Now, so much for him.

CB: Why did you do *Rodeo* for Ballet Russe [de Monte Carlo] rather than Ballet Theatre?

ADM: Well, you see, Lucia would never give me a contract. I never had a place in my theatre, never. The following year I was called in to do *Three Virgins* on two weeks' notice, because they needed a ballet for Lucia. Pleasant kept saying, "I'm not going to let you choreograph for yourself. You have to choreograph for other people." And I was whining and kicking, and he said, "No, you'll never learn to cho-

reograph, you never will on yourself alone."

CB: You went to Denham because of Gerry Sevastianov?

ADM: They wouldn't give me any place in the whole thing at all. And I begged to have Sybil Shearer, for instance, brought in, who is the funniest woman I know on two legs outside of me, and together we were excruciating. And Hugh Laing tried to get her. She was a modern dancer, and Lucia wouldn't even consider her. I said she's one of the biggest technicians I've ever seen in my life. She just doesn't get on point. She should have played The Devil once. It wasn't like Dennis Nahat, but it was the very living heart and soul of Bosch. But Lucia wouldn't dream of it. She was very, very orthodox. But Lucia was herself a brilliant comedienne.

CB: As a complete digression—interesting that you should mention Nahat—I never saw Eugene Loring do the original.

ADM: Oh, no?

CB: I saw Michael Kidd, who was very good.

ADM: Not very.

CB: But Nahat . . . there are some times when a role comes into focus in quite an incredible way.

ADM: Absolutely.

CB: And Nahat is an incredible dancer.

ADM: He is the best one that ever did it. Lazovsky did it for quite a long time, you know, he wasn't good. What Jerry [Robbins] did as The Youth was outrageous. You can't imagine how much that used to get screams and whistles.

CB: Actually, Jerry originally did it in Covent Garden in 1946. Or was it Kriza?

ADM: It was Kriza. Kriza couldn't get the counts. They're very tricky. They're all on the wrong count, you see. Every step is arranged so that you drop a stitch and pick it up and go on. Jerry was really marvelous. His eyebrows are so funny.

CB: Well, he was a super dancer, wasn't he?

ADM: He was like Massine.

CB: He *was* like Massine. He looked like Massine as well, as a kid.

ADM: His sense of timing! Oh, nobody's done *Fancy Free. Nobody.*

CB: Except Nahat. Nahat is very good in that part. Dennis has done that very well. And Feld did it rather well, actually. Because Feld has the same sort of deep, Jewish Carmen Miranda intensity. There's no doubt that Jerry was very, very good. I suppose it was Kriza who did The Youth next.

ADM: Yes, it was. He was all right, too, you know, but not super. That's a star role, you see. Those were little roles, and dancers think if you can't get on your points and into a tutu properly, then of course you can play comedy in the De Mille ballets. The things I've witnessed!

CB: Tell me, when Gerry Sevastianov said he didn't want *Rodeo* for Ballet Theatre, you took it to Ballet Russe? And after that was *Oklahoma*?

ADM: Immediately, and the world changed for me, of course.

CB: And then Ballet Theatre asked you back.

ADM: Well, they wanted a comedy ballet for Lucia. And I was supposed to do *Tally Ho*, and that was supposed to be immediately after *Oklahoma*! And then I was scheduled to do *One Touch of Venus*, which I did do in September, and then my husband was shipped. I followed him to the staging area, which was against the law, against marshal law, I did it secretly and hid out in St. Louis. That was a rather dreadful week. I said good-bye to him every morning, not knowing if I'd ever see him again or not. And sometimes he'd come home and sometimes he wouldn't and then one night he didn't. Word just came—one of his soldiers telephoned. He said, "You are to go to New York." Then he shipped out for the duration. Well, I was not in good condition to carry on with a light, fluffy comedy with a major war going on. I don't mean the European conflict, I mean Dolin and Hugh Laing fighting to death on my chest.

CB: Of course. They were doing the leading roles, weren't they?

ADM: And in two different schools of performing. And Dolin got so he absolutely hated me, just hated me. And I was afraid. I had hysterics the night before the opening and called up a friend and said, "He's going to drop me. I know he's going to drop me." Oh, that man. It was very funny, because well, I was a pretty good dancer, but I wasn't a ballerina, and I couldn't run and land on his shoulder . . . I had a lot of skirts on, too. Dolin's rather a sweet man, though. Do you know that? He's done very kind things. And the minute he knew I was crippled, he was very kind to me. He's been very kind and loyal many times. He took Spessivtzeva under his wing, he took care of her.

CB: Dolin . . . I remember him as a performer very

well. I remember him probably in the latter years of his career. . . . Well, he was still pretty good. I saw him first in 1948 and even then he was an incredible presence and quite a strong technician.

ADM: Oh, yes.

CB: And you could imagine then what he must have been like twenty years earlier.

ADM: Well, he had two or three styles. I used to see him down the Kings Road in one of those awful vaudeville houses, where there'd be four a day doing a dance, a Spanish dance, on full point.

CB: *Bolero.*

ADM: With a decolletage just below the navel.

CB: He used to go down on his knees. As Albrecht, he would jump and then go smash on his knees, and you thought, my god, he's going to hurt himself. And he used to do that in his bolero.

ADM: I worked on *Tally Ho* all across the United States, and that was not a finished ballet, just never was. And then when we got to New York, finally, I danced the lead and I was very funny. It takes a rather mature comedienne.

CB: One of the things I remember about *Tally Ho* is those lovely names of the characters—Lady No Better Than She Should Be and Two Ladies Somewhat Worse?

ADM: That's right. Oh, I want to do it again and put the proper ending on it. We had such comediennes, Karnilova and Muriel Bentley, those rich, good girls. They were real gutsy.

CB: Laing was very good in it as well.

ADM: Very. Funny.

CB: And *Tally Ho* had lovely decor. It was very pretty.

ADM: It was Motley. Miraculous costumes. I think all her costumes are just the ultimate in economy and suggestiveness and color. You could have eaten the color with a spoon, it was so good.

CB: Tell me, then you went on and this was . . .

ADM: Now we're up to 1945. It's no longer just beginning. It's a company.

CB: The company has really begun, and you are really very deeply involved in it.

ADM: Never with any continuity. It was always ballet by ballet by ballet. I did a ballet for the Jooss Ballet. That was earlier.

CB: *Drums Sound in Hackensack*

ADM: Terrible, terrible, terrible. But it was an interesting experience. There were good moments in it. But, with a group of starving dancers. And of course, the German sense of humor is not mine.

CB: No. No. Sigurd Leeder was never very funny.

ADM: Believe me. I'd suddenly stop and just say "This'll kill you. Now let me tell you." And they'd say "Count it, please." I finally got Sybil Shearer to come down from upper New York State and said just sit there and tell me, am I funny or not?

CB: This was of course a time when modern dance and classic ballet were at odds with one another. I mean, you must have found, to an extent—you already mentioned the concept that you are not a classic ballerina—you must have found when you started that there was a terrific amount of opposition.

ADM: Oh, my god!

CB: I mean, now Glen Tetley can come in and do choreography, and no one thinks of Glen as being a modern dancer as such.

ADM: Well, the moderns were quite aggressive and quite self-conscious and militant because they were fighting. The *Dance Observer*, which was Louis Horst's organ, was for Martha Graham. (It was her own personal house organ.) I suggested, when I came back from England at one point, that they get a friend of mine, Ramon, to write the dance criticism, and I said, "It will have to be ballet because there isn't any other dancing in England." Well, they said they wouldn't have ballet dancing mentioned in their pages. I said, "Oh, come on now, That's stuffy." And, they said, "No, we won't. We just don't believe in it." That was the point of view of the Graham School at that moment.

CB: Absolutely. I always remember when Martha finally admitted that her ballets were ballets. They were not to be called dances. They were not to be called plays, and she was not supposed to be a dramatist. And I could always see her biting the bullet because it happened in England, and I remember someone very daringly saying, "Do you wish your works to be called ballets or do you wish them to be called dances?" And she looked very hard, and a shadow passed over her face, and she said, "I think they ought to be called ballets." This would be about twelve years ago—something like that—fifteen years ago, perhaps. But when did you do *The Harvest According*? That would have been about 1952?

ADM: 1953. It's gone.

CB: Yes, it's a pity that's gone.

ADM: Lucia lost it. I was doing my own company, and I couldn't do anything about *Harvest*, and she just made no effort to keep it at all.

CB: In my opinion, it was a very nice work, a good work.

ADM: It had a good score.

CB: Lovely decor, that very orange decor. Your Broadway musical, it's a marvelous dance. Was it partly based on *Bloomer Girl*?

ADM: The Civil War ballet was. That's the only part. It was other music. The Virgil Thomson score was an amalgam of old hymns and his cello concerto.

CB: You've always been associated with the concept of Americana.

ADM: Not at all, pre-America. It came gradually. First of all there were genre studies of dancers and their lives. That's all the Degas stuff I did in London. And then the eighteenth century. I had a whole line of eighteenth century and earlier, but they were mainly eighteenth-century dances. And I did one Americana piece in each program over in England, because no one else was doing them. I'm tired of it now.

CB: Really?

ADM: Oh, sure.

CB: Do you think Ballet Theatre should have had a more obviously American . . . impact?

ADM: No. I think it's had it. I don't think you're American if you put a sunbonnet on.

CB: No, I agree with you.

ADM: I think Jerry is American. Just the way I think Antony is English, and it's in the quality of thinking, the quality of humor.

CB: Yes, when you look at those Chopin pieces that Jerry does, they all come out American. They'll be danced by a couple of Russians, but they'll come out American.

ADM: Those I was disappointed in.

CB: Were you? Those *Other Dances*? I liked them, I really did.

ADM: I know the music very well.

CB: *Dances at a Gathering*.

ADM: I liked that. I happen to know the music awfully well. You can't lean too heavily on the music and say this is fine just because the music is fine.

CB: No, of course.

ADM: I think *Les Noces* is a masterpiece.

CB: It's incredible, isn't it? It's a great piece. What would you have liked to have seen Ballet Theatre do, or do you think it did what it should have done?

ADM: Well, I think it has wasted a lot of time doing a lot of nonsense. And I'm not crazy about it doing all the big fluffy pieces from the Russian repertory, but I'm told that's just plain box office in the sticks.

CB: I don't. But then it's very much part of my childhood.

ADM: Well, that performance in Covent Garden with Margot Fonteyn with the original Oliver Messel designs was ravishing. Somehow this wasn't. Except that Makarova is exquisite. There's an aura around that girl. And their *Swan Lake*, I don't happen to like the choreography or the arrangement. Who did the choreography this time?

CB: David Blair.

ADM: I didn't like it. I don't think it's musical.

CB: It's really the same as the Royal Ballet. It is as near as you can get to the original St. Petersburg production.

ADM: Well, it's not musical, and I just can't bear it.

CB: How would you have liked Ballet Theatre to have gone?

ADM: I think it's very healthy. Now, I don't know what would happen if anything happened to Lucia. Because there's nobody in that company who has her catholic taste. You see, everyone, even Tudor, who has enormous taste, is really besotted with his or her own concerns.

CB: How about Oliver Smith? How do you see Oliver?

ADM: He has very good taste, but he hasn't got anything like Lucia's force of character. I don't think he would have the drive. I don't think he has enough staying power. Also, I don't think you should be an active choreographer and also be the head of a company of this size. Absolutely not.

CB: I agree with you. How did you feel growing up in Ballet Theatre and growing up in American ballet generally as a woman? Did you feel it was difficult? You have occasionally written about this, but did you feel that there was a prejudice?

ADM: A prejudice in Ballet Theatre, or what?

CB: Well, in ballet generally.

ADM: Or in the outside world against ballet? What do you mean?

CB: Not the outside world against ballet, but against women in ballet. Did you ever feel it was more difficult being a woman than it would have been had you been a man?

ADM: No.

CB: It's interesting that so many of the people who created ballet, certainly in the Anglo-American world, were women.

ADM: They all were the creators, the founders. Well, I think it's because the men who would have been their counterparts and perhaps more effective were doing other things. This is a despised field.

CB: It was, but not now, don't you think?

ADM: Well, it's the most popular field there is in the theatre. This is second to tennis and baseball, but it's more popular than anything, except movies perhaps.

CB: But this is something in which there's been an incredible change.

ADM: Oh, just incredible. Well, when I was a girl and I'd meet anyone, "What are you?" "I'm a dancer" —well, of course, I know nothing about dancing, and they'd look down at my legs and expect to find them thick and awful, and then that's all the interest they had in that. They used to inflame me to rage.

CB: What are the things that pleased you most with your association with Ballet Theatre?

ADM: Lucia has always been stalwart, steady. My hat's off to her. Rain, cold, windy, or still, she just goes on and that's very strong character. You see, I think you should be judged by your best works, not by just what you consistently turn out, because that has to do with all kinds of things. And there are reasons why works don't turn out well. But the best works are what you have to be judged by.

CB: I agree. That's true. That's what's going to last.

ADM: And the rest won't last. They'll just blow away.

CB: How many works by Petipa have lasted? Very few.

ADM: And they're all the same piece, anyway. Bournonville, I think, is just enchanting.

CB: Yes, I do too.

ADM: And he lasts.

CB: But only about eight ballets.

ADM: Perrot's parts of *Giselle* are ravishing.

CB: One ballet, that's all that's left.

ADM: Well, but that's accident, don't you think? How do you know that only one's lasted? They all stole like mad. Saint-Léon put his name on everything.

CB: And anyway, nowadays choreographers have a better chance. There's notation, there's film. I'm amazed at the similarities in *Les Sylphides* all over the world. It's incredible. I know they vary, but every time Fokine himself did it, they varied. But it is incredible how similar they are. It's incredible how much some of the Balanchine ballets are consistent throughout everywhere. And it's amazing how now people have a much closer regard, it seems to me, for a choreographer than they had.

ADM: Well, I think they do.

CB: Much closer, which is a good thing, I think, because it's the basis of a repertory, and it means that all these new companies that are emerging everywhere can have a repertory of old works just the same as an opera company would normally have a repertory of old works. It's very important, it seems to me.

ADM: Well, it's the whole reason why things are looking better.

Jerome Robbins

Jerome Robbins has never been associated with Ballet Theatre for any extended period of time, and yet along with Antony Tudor and Agnes de Mille he seems to be an archetypal Ballet Theatre choreographer. Curiously enough, Robbins has only contributed five ballets to the repertory, among which are the 1976 revival of *Other Dances* for Natalia Makarova and Mikhail Baryshnikov and *Interplay*, also a revival. Robbins danced with the company from 1940 until 1948, and his career had its first major impetus with his work for Ballet Theatre, for which also he created his first ballet.

Jerome Robbins started dancing in his late teens. He first studied modern dance with teachers who were strongly influenced by Isadora Duncan, and in the first company he danced in, he appeared alongside of the great modern dancer José Limon. He took up classic ballet simply because a perceptive teacher, Gluck Sandor, told Robbins shortly before World War II that classic ballet was going to be the coming thing. The man was so right—Robbins's career was fixed; and that teacher, presumably without especial forethought, has changed the course of American ballet.

The influences on Robbins were numerous. He recognizes Gluck Sandor as a major influence, and, of course, when Robbins first joined Ballet Theatre,

JACK MITCHELL

he came into the orbit of a number of important choreographers, including Antony Tudor, Leonide Massine, Agnes de Mille, David Lichine, Bronislava Nijinska, and—then in his last years—Michel Fokine.

Another early mentor of Robbins at Ballet Theatre was George Balanchine, the choreographer with whom he ultimately made his major career helping to form the New York City Ballet. When Balanchine was working with Ballet Theatre, Robbins would ask to sit in on his rehearsals, because he was interested in seeing how he worked, though Robbins himself had already scored his first major successes with *Fancy Free* and *Interplay*, and had moved into the Broadway ambit that was to provide a second home for him for twenty years. One day Robbins met Balanchine on a boat. Robbins tells it: "I think it was the summer after Leonard Bernstein and myself with Betty Comden and Adolph Green had first done *On The Town*, my first Broadway musical. I went up to Nantucket and came back and found myself on a boat with Balanchine. I asked if I could sit and talk with him, and he explained choreography to me. He did it in just two or three sentences, and it was so illuminating to my head, it was just like the light had

93

been turned on about what choreography was really about. That was a unique influence right then and there." When I was talking with Robbins, he never elaborated on "what choreography was really about," but then I suspect that it is difficult for nonchoreographers to understand unless they think of choreography as songs without words.

In terms not only of his personal career as a choreographer but also of his beginnings with Ballet Theatre, Robbins speaks of Balanchine as a major influence. But it was a Balanchine who was then involved with Broadway shows. I asked Robbins whether after his early ballet training he then joined Ballet Theatre. He replied "No, not its first season. From those early classic lessons I went into musical comedy and danced in the choruses of shows for about two years. That is where I first met Mr. Balanchine. He did a show called *Great Lady*, and in the chorus of that show were Alicia Alonso, Nora Kaye, Paul Godkin, and other dancers who later moved on to ballet, but they also had a *pas de sept*, and in that group were André Eglevsky, Leda Anchutina, Annabelle Lyon, and most of the stars in what was then the American Ballet Company. This was my first exposure to genuine classic choreography. There were only two people who got into that musical who were not members of the School of American Ballet. I was one of them. I joined Ballet Theatre in 1940 or 1941, I am not sure which. It sounds fast, but then I did study very hard, taking three or four classes a day. I joined Ballet Theatre in their second year and just stayed with them."

One of the choreographers who initially took great interest in Robbins was Fokine. Robbins says, "Fokine encouraged me tremendously and gave me things to dance. He taught me Petrouchka—although, in all fairness, I must say that I was the third Petrouchka in the rehearsal line of Petrouchkas when he first taught it to Ballet Theatre; but I was there through all the rehearsals, and he was very inspiring to work with."

The puppet Petrouchka was Robbins's first truly major part. "I first saw the ballet way up at the top of the old Met in 1937 or 1938. It must have been the De Basil company. It was so high up there that you could see down behind the puppet booths, and you could see the dancers come in and get ready. I was rather disappointed that the ballet did not live up to what I had read about it."

The way Robbins worked at his interpretation of Petrouchka seems typical of his meticulousness and sense of artistic rightness. "I looked at the pictures of Petrouchka and decided he was painted as badly as he was because he probably wouldn't see very well, hear well, and generally had a hard time for focusing; so the studies I did were all about how he would physically relate to everything. I would go into the puppet booth and try to imagine the first time he had found his consciousness there—trying to go at it as an actor, so that I knew everything I could about him. I was very intense about it in those days!"

Although Robbins had begun choreographing chamber works before 1944, *Fancy Free* was, of course, his first work for American Ballet Theatre. Recalling *Fancy Free*, Robbins said: "Well, I had sort of been propagandizing Ballet Theatre to let me do ballets, and when I think about them, they really were rather ambitious. They were four-act, full-length ballets, with mostly Americana themes somehow or other. I think it was Anatole Chujoy who said: 'Why don't you get together a small ballet with a few people?' so that's what I had to do, think of a small ballet with a few people.

"And then a woman named Mary Hunter, who is now one of the directors of the Stratford Theatre in Connecticut, suggested to me in a conversation one night, 'Why don't you base a ballet on a picture like, maybe, *The Fleet's In?*' I thought, 'well, that's an idea. I went off and figured out a whole story and submitted it. I think someone wasn't able to do a ballet who was supposed to—so, by a freak chance it was accepted.

"Vincent Persichetti suggested I show the scenario to someone he knew named Bernstein and gave me his address. I went to that address in New York and there was nothing there, not even a house. Oliver Smith said he knew where Lennie was, so we went to see him, and I gave him the scenario, and he played me some of the music, and that was the beginning of the collaboration. When we finally met, I was swept into a new world.

"Oliver Smith, who was already established as a designer, said to me, 'I hear you're doing a ballet and I'd like to design it.' " *Fancy Free* made both composer and choreographer famous overnight.

According to Robbins, the success of this was a complete surprise, since no one had seen it. In those days there were no dress rehearsals, and word of mouth was slow to leak out. "By the time the reviews came in, we were terrified to get on stage again. I remember we all fell down at the second performance. One at a time, at different places in the ballet, our feet just went off from underneath us."

Fancy Free was followed the next year by *Interplay*, which received its first performance on June 1, 1945. The music was Morton Gould's *American Concertette* and the decor was by Carl Kent. The ballet was presented as part of Billy Rose's *Concert Varieties* at the Ziegfeld Theatre in New York. In the first cast were Janet Reed, Muriel Bentley, Bettina Rosai, Roszika Sabo, John Kriza, Jerome Robbins, Michael Kidd, and Erik Kristen. Later on, it was taken into the repertory of Ballet Theatre, receiving its first performance with them on October 17, 1945. Melissa Hayden replaced Rosai, Fernando Alonso replaced Robbins, Harold Lang replaced Kidd, and Tommy Rall replaced Kristen. The decor was by Oliver Smith, and the costumes were by Irene Sharaff. The ballet has no theme but celebrates with its jazzy rhythms the vitality of American youth.

The same team who produced *Fancy Free* again collaborated on *Facsimile*, which premiered at the Broadway Theatre on October 24, 1946. The principal roles were taken by Nora Kaye, John Kriza, and Robbins himself. Later on, Hugh Laing took over the role Robbins played. The original program quoted Santiago Ramón y Cajal: "Small inward treasure does he possess who to feel alive needs every hour the tumult of the street, the emotion of the theatre, and the small talk of society." A disturbing but fascinating ballet with psychological undertones, it was not retained in the repertory. The time is long overdue for its revival.

After *Facsimile*, Robbins devoted his time to the New York City Ballet, where he created a long string of works, and to Broadway, for which he created such masterpieces of the musical theatre as *West Side Story* and *Fiddler on the Roof*.

His return to Ballet Theatre came on March 30, 1965. For ten years Robbins had wanted to do *Les Noces*. He says: "As a matter of fact, I was supposed to do *Les Noces* in Spoleto the first time I was invited there. And then they found out that they couldn't get it together. . . . It wasn't a spring-off of *Fiddler*. My conferences with Stravinsky about it predate all of that. I am enormously proud of my ballet and have never regretted doing my own version, as has sometimes been said. When I saw Nijinska's, I was so deeply impressed and full of admiration for her version that I knew if I had seen hers first, it would have been impossible to choreograph my own. I had to have it clean to myself to be able to do it, and if I had seen her version and her solution of things first, I would have had a hard time with my interpretations. In other words, it would have been hard not to have been influenced." *Les Noces* is indeed a major contribution to the American Ballet Theatre repertory in its scope and choreographic imagination and seems to inspire the company whenever they dance it.

In the summer of 1976 at a gala performance held at the Metropolitan Opera House to benefit the New York Public Library, the hit of the evening was a miniature for two dancers, Natalia Makarova and Mikhail Baryshnikov, created by Robbins to the music of Chopin. Chopin had also inspired several of Robbins's earlier ballets, most notably *Dances at a Gathering*, choreographed for the New York City Ballet in 1969. These latest lovely folk-flavored solos and *pas de deux*, entitled simply *Other Dances*, have now been taken into the repertory of the company with the original dancers.

It is, however, twelve years since the creation of *Les Noces*, Robbins's last full-scale ballet for American Ballet Theatre. Let us hope another will soon be on the way.

Current
Repertory

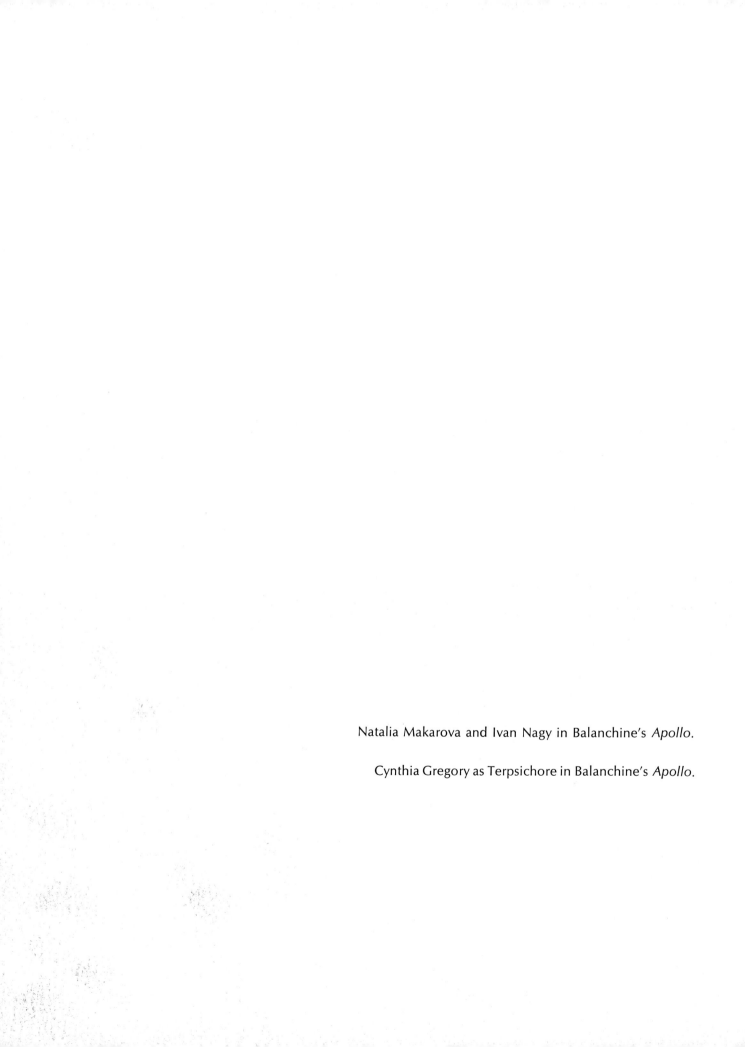

Natalia Makarova and Ivan Nagy in Balanchine's *Apollo*.

Cynthia Gregory as Terpsichore in Balanchine's *Apollo*.

BIL LEIDERSDORF

Ivan Nagy, Kim Highton, Natalia Makarova, Nanette Glushak in Balanchine's *Apollo*.

Terry Orr and Marianna Tcherkassky in *At Midnight*.

Bruce Marks in Eliot Feld's *At Midnight*.

Ivan Nagy, Eleanor D'Antuono, and Ted Kivitt in *Etudes*.

Fernando Bujones in *Etudes*.

Fernando Bujones in *Etudes*.

Lucia Chase, Gayle Young, and Sallie Wilson in Agnes de Mille's *Fall River Legend*.

Jerome Robbins's *Fancy Free*.

Agnes de Mille's *The Four Marys* with Judith Lerner, Paul Sutherland, Cleo Quitman, Judith Jamison, Glory Van Scott, and Carmen de Lavallade.

David Lichine's *Graduation Ball*.

On the following pages, Lupe Serrano, Royes Fernandez, and Lucia Chase in Kenneth MacMillan's *Las Hermanas*.

JACK MITCHELL

Dianne Richards and Royes Fernandez in Tudor's *Lilac Garden*.

Birgit Cullberg's *Miss Julie*.

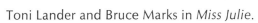

Toni Lander and Bruce Marks in *Miss Julie*.

113

Toni Lander, Bruce Marks, Royes Fernandez, and Sallie Wilson in José Limon's
The Moor's Pavane.

Erin Martin in Robbins's *Les Noces*.

Natalia Makarova and Paolo Bortoluzzi in Tudor's *Pillar of Fire*.

Sallie Wilson and Gayle Young in Tudor's *Pillar of Fire*.

Jonas Kage and Martine van Hamel in Alvin Ailey's *The River*.

Natalia Makarova and Erik Bruhn in *The River*.

Christine Sarry as The Cowgirl in De Mille's *Rodeo*.

BIL LEIDERSDORF

Christine Sarry and Terry Orr in De Mille's *Rodeo*.

LOUIS PÉRES

122

Carla Fracci in Tudor's *Romeo and Juliet*.

LOUIS PÉRES

Gelsey Kirkland in Tudor's *Shadowplay*.

Fernando Bujones in Tudor's *Shadowplay*.

Cynthia Gregory in Peter Darrell's *Tales of Hoffmann*.

Eliot Feld and Daniel Levins in Feld's *The Soldier's Tale*.

Dennis Nahat, Christine Sarry, Ruth Mayer, and Sallie Wilson in De Mille's
Three Virgins and a Devil.

LOUIS PÉRES

Cynthia Gregory and Fernando Bujones in Tudor's *Undertow*.

Ivan Nagy, Ted Kivitt, John Prinz, and Paolo Bortoluzzi in Anton Dolin's *Variations for Four*.

The
Dancers

American Ballet Theatre is a dancers' company—always has been and presumably always will be. It started that way in 1940, and it remains that way in 1976. Most of the great dancers of the Western world would have at one time appeared with Ballet Theatre, either as regular members of the troupe, as guest artists, or occasionally simply taking part in one of the innumerable gala performances that over the years Ballet Theatre has made something of a speciality of the house.

Dancers enjoy working with Ballet Theatre simply because the varied, eclectic nature of the repertory gives them more of a chance than with most companies to show off their talents. The other two major classic companies in the United States, New York City Ballet and the Joffrey Ballet, both list their dancers alphabetically, although the Balanchine company does admit to having principals. (It was, however, a departing ballerina from City Ballet, Maria Tallchief, who is said to have snorted on leaving: "I don't mind being listed alphabetically, but I won't stand being treated alphabetically.") Stars with Ballet Theatre are for the most part cosseted and nurtured.

The star system has some disadvantages, and the guest star system, whereby famous name guest artists are brought in to bolster up seasons in such cities as New York, Washington, D.C., or Los Angeles, can indeed be criticized as unfair and downright discouraging to loyal members of the company who bear the brunt of the less glamorous touring. Yet for all this, these transient comets do add something to the company's specific tone and flavor. They also provide the public with something the public clearly wants and also offer the home team the very real stimulus of front-rank competition.

In the sketches that follow I have made a distinction between what might be called regular guest artists, who have, as it were, put down roots with the company, and occasional guest artists, who may have appeared for a number of seasons but cannot be only associated with the company. For example, during the past season Paolo Bortoluzzi, Richard Cragun, Hideo Fugakawa, Vladimir Gelvan, Marcia Haydée, Yoko Morishita, Rudolf Nureyev, and Lynn Seymour all appeared with the company. But as with Michael Denard of a few seasons back, few of them seem likely to establish the kind of permanent relations offered by, say, Mikhail Baryshnikov, Erik Bruhn, and Natalia Makarova.

It would be tempting here also to include sketches of some of the great dancers of the past—and there have been so many, not only those from the beginning of the company's history, such as Nora Kaye, André Eglevsky, Igor Youskevitch, Jerome Robbins, Anton Dolin, Irina Baronova, Alicia Markova, John Kriza, as well as many from more recent days, such as Toni Lander, Lupe Serrano, Royes Fernandez, Bruce Marks, Scott Douglas, and Ruth Ann Koesun. It is a temptation that has had to be resisted, for this is not really a history of Ballet Theatre but a lightning impression of the company as it is today, with a certain amount of background showing how it got there. But those dancers will never be forgotten, nor will the part they have played in making Ballet Theatre history and forming that fugitive but very real Ballet Theatre style.

In the sketches that follow I have followed the company practice and with one exception, followed alphabetical order. The exception, in case you are wondering why she has not been mentioned before, is that veteran, heroine, and exile, Alicia Alonso.

Mikhail Baryshnikov

Baryshnikov was born in Riga, Latvia, of Russian parents on January 27, 1948. His father, a retired engineer, lives in Riga with Baryshnikov's stepmother.

Baryshnikov is one of the most perfect dancers of his time, a consummate classicist, yet also a dancer of tremendous dramatic power. He started dancing in Riga when he was twelve. His mother took him to the School of the Theatre Opera Ballet. He studied academic subjects as well as ballet; he started French and also began to play the piano. At one time he considered a career as a concert pianist, and he is a fine pianist even today.

Three years after starting in Riga he went with a group of young dancers to Leningrad. On his own initiative he applied for entrance at the great Vaganova School in Leningrad, the school of the Kirov Ballet; he was accepted and joined the class of Aleksander Pushkin, who previously had been the teacher and mentor of Rudolf Nureyev. It was in Pushkin's class, in the summer of 1967, that I first saw Baryshnikov dance. Russian friends had told me to watch out for him—but one hardly needed to be told. A few days later, I saw him on stage for the first time at the Kirov Theatre. He danced the *pas de deux* from Vainonen's old ballet *The Flames of Paris*, and he was brilliant.

His career swept on. He won prizes galore—at Varna, Bulgaria, and in the most prestigious dance competition in the world, Moscow. I saw him in class the following year. He was injured and disappointingly could not appear on stage, but we chatted, in pidgin French (him in French, me in pidgin), and I saw him dance once more in class.

He started to tour with the Kirov Ballet and soon became a star of considerable reputation. The next time I saw him dance was in London in 1970. He was with the Kirov Ballet dancing at the Royal Festival Hall—it was the season when Natalia Makarova defected. Baryshnikov was the hero of the season, not only for the astonishing grace and strength of his dancing, but also for a strangely evocative dramatic solo the Leningrad choreographer Leonid Jacobsen created for him, called *Vestris*. He has since danced it with Ballet Theatre, and with its dramatics and stylistic, impressionistic suggestion of eighteenth-century dance, it is one of the most unusual and effective solos ever made for a specific dancer. Soon he was the undisputed golden boy of the Kirov Ballet and had roles created for him, sharing, for instance, the eponymous role in Konstantin Sergeyev's *Hamlet* with Valery Panov. At this time he had not yet danced the major classic leads, but for

the fall of 1974 he had been invited by Yuri Grigorovich, artistic director of the Bolshoi Ballet, to go to Moscow as guest artist and dance his first Siegfried in *Swan Lake* and his first Albrecht in *Giselle*. It was not to be.

In the summer of 1974, he went with a rather shabby group of dancers drawn from both the Kirov and Bolshoi ballets, who were making a tour of Canada. On June 29, Baryshnikov walked out of the stage door of the O'Keefe Center in Toronto into a waiting car provided by friends. He instantly sought and was given political asylum by the Canadian government. Soon after, he made his first appearance in the West with the National Ballet of Canada, and he still keeps that company on his visiting list. Since then he has danced all over the Western world, but the companies he is most closely associated with are primarily American Ballet Theatre and secondarily, Britain's Royal Ballet.

Soon after Baryshnikov fled to the West, Sherwin Goldman, then president of the American Ballet Theatre Foundation, telephoned me in London, asking that he be put in touch with the young Russian, who was still lying low in Canada. This I happened to be able to arrange, and almost immediately Baryshnikov made his debut with Ballet Theatre at the New York State Theater. Unfortunately I missed that debut—he danced in *Giselle* with Natalia Makarova —but I returned to New York a few days later to see him as dazzling as ever in the *Don Quixote pas de deux*.

Since his arrival in the West, Baryshnikov has had quite a number of works mounted on him, beginning with John Butler's *Medea*, a ballet set to Samuel Barber's music for Baryshnikov and Carla Fracci, originally given at the Spoleto Festival in 1975. Later, Twyla Tharp created *Push Comes to Shove* for him, then there was *Hamlet Connotations* by John Neumeier, and probably most important of all, that fascinating Jerome Robbins duet, *Other Dances*, which was created for him and Makarova. He has also appeared in such varied roles as The Green Skater in Ashton's *Les Patineurs*, The Boy with the Matted Hair in Tudor's *Shadowplay*, The Young Man in Roland Petit's *Le Jeune Homme et La Mort*, and The Spectre in Fokine's *Le Spectre de la Rose*. And, of course, most of the classic leads, both with Ballet Theatre and, more recently, the Royal Ballet.

His dancing is full of fire and ice; it has great passion and displays a surprisingly cheeky sense of humor. He is a force in the dance world and is at this moment poised to take a new step by staging for Ballet Theatre his version of *The Nutcracker*. Whether he has a career as a ballet master and choreographer remains to be seen. He certainly has a career ahead of him as a dancer.

Karena Brock

There are some dancers who are the backbone of any company, and I suppose Brock is one of these. She was born in Los Angeles, but her earliest ballet training was in the Ballet Department of Texas Christian University in Fort Worth, Texas. Later she worked with Dorothy Perkins in Kansas City, Missouri, and later still she was back in Los Angeles, studying with the former Ballet Russe [de Monte Carlo] stars, David Lichine and Tatiana Riabouchinska.

She first performed with a company called Ballet Celeste and then with the Netherlands National Ballet before joining American Ballet Theatre in 1963. Once in Ballet Theatre her progress was steady —she was made a soloist in 1968 and promoted to a principal dancer in 1973. She is married to another ABT principal, Ted Kivitt, and she often makes guest artist appearances with him across the country.

Brock has had some good roles over the years, and to all of them she has brought a certain bright sensibility. Although stylistically she is not a perfect classicist, she does have personality. She had a personal success as Helen in *Helen of Troy* (she was one of the few ballet Helens, Diana Adams was another one, pretty enough to "have launched a thousand ships") and has done well in the quadruple role in Peter Darrell's full-evening *Tales of Hoffmann*, as well as in the taxing virtuoso role, created for Toni Lander, in Harald Lander's *Etudes*.

Erik Bruhn

Erik Bruhn, although I presume a guest artist, is today American Ballet Theatre's senior member. In his day, which was not so long ago, Bruhn was indisputably the greatest male dancer in the world, incomparable, in a class apart. He is still a wonderful character dancer and a strict perfectionist. He is also an important teacher, coach, and general ballet savant.

Bruhn was born in Copenhagen on October 3, 1928. When he was nine he auditioned with about three hundred other children for a place in Denmark's Royal Ballet School. He was one of the twelve taken. From then on his life revolved around the Royal Danish Ballet, and in 1947 he graduated from the school and was instantly taken into the company. During the war years, when Denmark was occupied by Nazi Germany, Bruhn grew up in a claustrophobic atmosphere. He really wanted to escape. Everyone told him he was wonderful. Indeed he was wonderful—but he needed to find out how wonderful outside of Copenhagen. That same year he went to London. It was a fantastic time for dance. He studied with two great Russian teachers, Stanislas Idzikowski and, more particularly, Fonteyn's teacher, Vera Volkova, who ironically enough was to spend the last twenty years of her life heading the Royal Danish Ballet School. In 1948 Bruhn saw everything available: dance, theater, opera. He decided to take a leave of absence from the Danish Ballet and to try his luck in Britain. He joined a new British company called the Metropolitan Ballet. It was a company that made very little impact, but it did have the distinction of introducing Bruhn and the ballerina Svetlana Beriosova to the world at large. I remember them dancing *Le Spectre de la Rose* together, and it was magic.

Right from the beginning it was evident that Bruhn was an enormous talent. In 1949 he was appointed *solodancer* to the Royal Danish Ballet (the equivalent of principal dancer) at what was then an almost unbelievably young age. Perhaps it was an attempt to keep him in Denmark. It failed. The following season he went off to join Ballet Theatre, and from then on, although this peregrinating artist found many temporary homes and refuges, in some strange way, Ballet Theatre became his base.

He joined as a comparatively junior member, and he had, considering his genius, a comparatively rough time in rising to the top. And, of course, he was always going away. He was a great joiner, but also a great leaver. It was a strange, meteoric career, played under so many different auspices. Bruhn never really cut himself off completely from Denmark. He is still a Dane, he has a house in Copenhagen, and just with the nod of his head he could probably become director of the Royal Danish Ballet. Some of his finest performances have been given with the Danes, but he has always been a guest artist in his own land. At ballet festivals, at important engagements in London or New York, Bruhn would rush into his native company, prove himself the impeccable Bournonville stylist of his day, and then disappear to Ballet Theatre, the Stuttgart Ballet, the Harkness Ballet, the Australian Ballet, the National Ballet of Canada, the Royal Swedish Ballet, New York City Ballet (he had two stormy seasons with George Balanchine, where they both agreed to admire and differ), or Britain's Royal Ballet (he had one extraordinary season in 1962 with this company).

He and Rudolf Nureyev, his heir apparent as the world's greatest male dancer and by then his best friend, were both engaged as guest artists for one sensational season. Nureyev was dancing with Margot Fonteyn, Bruhn was dancing with Nadia Nerina. Bruhn was 33, and he probably never danced better, technically at least, before or since. He was almost outrageously perfect.

Then he danced a lot with the Canadians, formed a marvelous and very fulfilling partnership with the Italian ballerina Carla Fracci, and for some years was the trump card of Ballet Theatre. He also began to choreograph and to mount ballets. In 1967 he became the director of the Royal Swedish Ballet, which did not seem to affect his performance schedule with Ballet Theatre. After three somewhat unhappy years he left the Swedes, and in 1971, following an injury, he retired quite suddenly, mid-season, from Ballet Theatre.

At the end of this part of his career, Bruhn had started a new and fruitful partnership with Natalia Makarova, and he not only danced the classics with her, they also created the "Giggling Rapids" duet in Alvin Ailey's ballet of Duke Ellington's *The River* and the leading roles in Ulf Gadd's version of Bartók's *The Miraculous Mandarin*. Leaving Ballet Theatre he joined the National Ballet of Canada as its associate producer, and in this capacity he has staged *Swan Lake*, *Coppélia*, and Bournonville's *La Sylphide*. It was in the summer of 1974 at the Metropolitan Opera House that he returned to the stage with the Canadians, playing the mime role in *La Sylphide* of Madge the Witch. That winter, Ballet Theatre persuaded him to come out of retirement to appear in its 35th Anniversary Gala, dancing excerpts from Birgit Cullberg's *Miss Julie* with Cynthia Gregory. He was a knockout, and after this success, he returned to Ballet Theatre. Since his return he has done many new roles—one stipulation he made was that he

would not dance anything in his former repertory— and he has become a different kind of artist. An injury received during the summer of 1976, dancing for the very first time in his career the title role in Fokine's *Petrouchka*, once again has put his dancing career in jeopardy. But Bruhn is first and foremost a man of the theatre who happened to be the most immaculate technician of his day. It is impossible to conceive that, while the immaculate technician has gone to teach, the man of the theatre will not demand a stage.

Fernando Bujones

I can never remember quite when it was I heard of Fernando Bujones, but I very well remember how. André Eglevsky, who was then teaching at the School of American Ballet, called up my wife, Patricia, and said he had a quite extraordinary Cuban boy in his class and would she like to come and take a look at him. She said yes—because Trish likes looking at new dancers almost as much as she likes looking at old dancers—and I recall talking to her after the class. "So what is the *wunderkind* like?" I asked. "He is fantastic—the nearest thing I have ever seen in class to Baryshnikov." This was years before Baryshnikov's defection, and Bujones was about fourteen at the time.

He was born in Miami, Florida, in 1956. (Some accounts suggest he was born in Cuba, but his family and his passport deny this.) His family, which is of Cuban origin, went to Havana soon after, and Bujones received his early training at Alicia Alonso's school in Havana. Following the Castro revolution, Bujones's family returned to the United States. Here Bujones studied at the New York Professional Children's School and, of course, at the School of American Ballet, first with Eglevsky and later with the Danish teacher Stanley Williams.

Even as a student his fame was spreading, particularly when he started to appear with the Eglevsky Ballet, sometimes partnering Gelsey Kirkland. He graduated from the School of American Ballet in 1972, and in June of that year he joined American Ballet Theatre. Wisely, I think, Lucia Chase insisted that the young man first enter the corps de ballet. This did not last long, however, for in 1973 he was made a soloist and in 1974 he was appointed a principal. He was an irresistible force.

In July of 1974 he went to Varna, Bulgaria, and competed in the International Ballet Competition, becoming the first American ever to win a gold medal. He was also given a special award for the highest technical achievement.

He is now at the beginning of a great career. Almost all of the leading classic prince roles have gone to him, and he has also appeared with great success in the Tudor repertory, dancing in such ballets as *Jardin aux Lilas*, *Shadowplay*, and *Undertow*. He has also had successes in Jerome Robbins's *Fancy Free* (he dances the Carmen Miranda-style sailor that Robbins himself originally created) and in many virtuoso roles, such as the leads in Balanchine's *Theme and Variations* and Lander's *Etudes*.

Bujones is a beautiful and very strong dancer, who has yet to find some special expression of his individuality. Yet already the signs are that this is coming. He needs more experience, and he will probably dance more and more outside of Ballet Theatre, although there is every indication that he will retain the American company as a home base. He has some twenty years of dancing ahead of him, and he has already come so far that how far he can go must be anybody's guess. But mine would be very far indeed.

William Carter

Bill Carter is one of the best character dancers in American ballet. For that matter, he is one of the best character dancers anywhere. He is happily versatile, quick, intelligent, and resourceful. He is also very experienced. He was born in Durant, Oklahoma, in 1936, and he had his early training from Carmelita Maracci in Los Angeles and from Cora Lene Duane in Oakland, California. He joined American Ballet Theatre in 1957, and although, at that time, he was there little more than a season, he was given lots of chances—including roles such as The First Sailor in *Fancy Free* and Robbins's own variation in *Interplay*. But in 1959 he left to join a Broadway musical *First Impressions*, which did not prove indelible. That

same year he joined the corps of New York City Ballet.

Two years later Balanchine promoted him to a soloist, and he was dancing roles such as The Fourth Movement in *Western Symphony*, The Fourth Movement in *Symphony in C*, and many other roles in the general repertory. In 1960 he created one of the four leading male roles in Balanchine's magnificent *Liebeslieder Walzer*, and in 1962 he created Demetrius in Balanchine's first full-evening creation, *A Midsummer Night's Dream*. That same year he was made a principal of the company, but immediately before the company's European and Russian tour, he left to form the First Chamber Dance Quartet, a chamber company with Lois Bewley, Nadine Revene, and Charles Bennett.

The First Chamber Dance Quartet was an important group and gave Carter ample opportunity to choreograph as well as to dance. However, in 1969, he rejoined Ballet Theatre as a soloist, and in 1976, after what some might have thought was an unduly long probationary period, he was finally appointed a principal dancer.

Although Carter probably finds his natural home with Ballet Theatre, he has always been something of a loner, something even of an outsider. For example, he is a remarkably skilled Spanish dancer—he used to dance with Maria Alba's Spanish Ballet and has trained with many of the Spanish teachers—and at Ballet Theatre galas, he is perfectly capable of electrifying an audience with a Spanish solo. He has also danced with Pearl Lang and was for a couple seasons, while still with Ballet Theatre, a principal dancer with the Martha Graham Company. He was marvelous in the Graham repertory, but eventually it became impossible for him to handle both Graham and Ballet Theatre, and his commitment to the latter proved the stronger.

His roles with Ballet Theatre have been innumerable. I recall him vividly in a number of roles in Alvin Ailey's *The River*, as The Champion Roper in De Mille's *Rodeo*, The Man She Must Marry in Tudor's *Jardin aux Lilas*, and in so many other parts throughout the repertory. Carter lends a certain maturity to a company that possibly, through no particular fault of its own, finds itself paying too much attention to youth. European companies have a tradition of the older dancer. It is a tradition we lack, and therefore Carter's presence and impact are all the more valuable.

Eleanor D'Antuono

If anyone can be said to be the grass roots of ABT today, it must surely be Eleanor D'Antuono. If anyone else is sick, she always seems to be there, and while she is not exactly played up by the company, by now she has done so much that she cannot exactly be played down. She was born in Cambridge, Massachusetts, in 1939, and was soon training in Boston with that famous teacher E. Virginia Williams, who is now the director of the Boston Ballet. D'Antuono danced with Williams's predecessor to the Boston Ballet, the New England Civic Ballet, and then in 1954 she joined the corps de ballet of the Ballet Russe de Monte Carlo. She moved her way up the company fairly rapidly, and then in the 1960–61 season she danced with the Joffrey Ballet, before joining American Ballet Theatre as a soloist in the fall of 1961. Two years later she was made a principal.

In the past fifteen years D'Antuono has virtually danced her way through the ABT repertory. Admittedly, not many dramatic roles have fallen to her, which could be a mistake, but all of the major classic repertory has come her way, and she has acquitted herself in it both admirably and consistently.

D'Antuono is regarded as reliable, which she certainly is. She is capable of some remarkable performances, particularly in soubrette roles, but also her Odette/Odile in *Swan Lake* can have some lovely moments. It is a pity that no one has really choreographed for her, and somehow, maybe it is because of that sometimes fatal quality of reliability, the company does not always seem to treat her as seriously as it might. She probably is never going to be a great ballerina, but she certainly does have a way with herself and a way with audiences. And she also is—what was that word—reliable. This is no small virtue in a repertory ballet company.

Carla Fracci

Although she has always been a guest artist, at least officially, Carla Fracci has appeared so frequently with ABT that she is at the very least an honorary member.

She was born in Milan on August 20, 1936, and she entered the ballet school of La Scala Milan at the age of ten, graduating in 1954. She was promoted to a soloist in 1956 and made a prima ballerina in 1958. She was a favorite dancer of the late John Cranko, who created his first version of *Romeo and Juliet* for her, and she first acquired international fame with the London Festival Ballet when in 1959 she made her debut in *Giselle* partnered by John Gilpin.

In 1960 and 1962 she was seen on United States television, and in 1963 she was a guest artist with Britain's Royal Ballet. In 1967 she danced in New York, partnered by Erik Bruhn, and for some years their partnership was one of the most significant in American dance. They appeared together in *Giselle*, *La Sylphide*, and *Coppélia*, and there was a wonderful rapport between them.

Subsequently, Fracci danced with Ballet Theatre in the classics and in the Tudor repertory, often partnered by her compatriot Paolo Bortoluzzi. She has a large following in America and rightly has always regarded American Ballet Theatre as her home away from home.

Cynthia Gregory

Of all the dancers of Ballet Theatre, Cynthia Gregory is among the most flamboyant and the most controversial. For example, who but Gregory, at the height of her career, would announce her premature retirement, go to the West Coast, remarry, and give up dancing all at the age of twenty-nine. But then, who would change her mind and, thank Heavens, return at the age of thirty. Gregory did.

She was born in Los Angeles on July 8, 1946. She began her ballet training with Eva Lorraine at the age of five and was on point at what many would consider the dangerously early age of six. Eva Lorraine ran the California Children's Ballet Company, and Gregory very soon acquired stage experience. Her major Californian teacher was, however, Carmelita Maracci.

At the age of fourteen, Gregory was given a scholarship by the Ford Foundation to work with Lew Christensen's San Francisco Ballet. Eventually she joined the San Francisco company, where, incidentally, she met her first husband, Terry Orr. Both Gregory and Orr appeared with the San Franciscan company on its one trip to New York, when it appeared at the New York State Theater in 1965. It was their ambition to dance with New York City Ballet, but around this time they saw some performances by American Ballet Theatre, liked what they saw, and decided to audition. They were taken into the company in 1965. In 1966 Gregory was made a soloist and nine months later elevated to a principal. She was very young but enormously promising, moreover she had the right ballerina temperament.

In 1967 the company appeared in San Francisco, and Gregory got the chance to dance Odette/Odile in *Swan Lake* for the first time. Her success was such that later the same year she made her New York debut in that role, and it has since become closely identified with her.

Like a number of American ballerinas—Suzanne Farrell springs to mind—Gregory is unusually tall. On point she stands over six feet. At first this seemed as though it could prove a disadvantage, but over the years she found ways of turning that majestic height into an advantage. Admittedly, one difficulty has always been the lack of suitable partners—there has been a succession of them, Bruce Marks, Ted Kivitt, Jonas Kage, Michael Denard, Vladimir Gelvan, to say nothing of Rudolf Nureyev. Perhaps the ideal partner would have been the Danish *premier danseur* of New York City Ballet, Peter Martins, but they have only danced together once at a gala.

Gregory's versatility as a classic ballerina is remarkable. She seems as much at home in *Giselle* or *La Sylphide* as in *Swan Lake* or *Raymonda*, while in ballets such as *Coppélia* or *La Fille Mal Gardée* she can offer sparkling soubrette performances that are really funny. The dramatic side to her dancing is one that has been somewhat neglected, perhaps particularly by modern choreographers. She was splendid for example in Tudor's *Undertow*, *Dark Elegies*, and *Jardin aux Lilas*, but no one, so far, seems to have thought of her as Hagar in *Pillar of Fire*.

Like many of the resident American members of Ballet Theatre, it seems that she has, on occasion, felt imperiled by the company's policy of importing guest artists. For her, this is particularly ridiculous, yet she seems to be a nervous, insecure woman, even in a profession where nervousness and insecurity are practically normal. This sabbatical away from dance may well have done Gregory good. From the age of five she had been dancing and dancing

and dancing. It was probably time to take the weight not just off her feet but off her mind.

The future for Gregory should be very rosy. Now entering her thirties she should be approaching her prime, and one hopes that the problem of the partner will eventually be solved to everyone's satisfaction. Now she has her first Aurora in the full-length version of *The Sleeping Beauty* immediately ahead of her, and it is to be hoped that modern choreographers will feel impelled to work with this beautiful all-American instrument. But perhaps she ought to be careful about restricting herself simply to Ballet Theatre in the future. It would be wonderful if an occasional exchange could be made with New York City Ballet—after all they are both public companies belonging, fundamentally, to the American people—so that Gregory could dance with Balanchine, and Suzanne Farrell could do some guest stints with Ballet Theatre. In any case, it is time for this gorgeous American swan queen to open up her wings a bit. She should be an international ballerina. America owes her to the world.

Gelsey Kirkland

Gelsey Kirkland was one of Balanchine's princesses —everyone I think expected that she would pursue her career with New York City Ballet. It seemed to be her destiny, and since she could presumably easily retrace her steps, perhaps it will so prove. But at the moment it seems that her star is moving toward Ballet Theatre.

She was born on December 29, 1953, in Bethlehem, Pennsylvania. She was a pupil of the School of American Ballet and a great favorite of André Eglevsky. Quite often she danced with the Eglevsky company on Long Island. She joined New York City Ballet in 1968, about the same time as her sister Johnna (born 1950), and her promotion was rapid. By 1970 she was a soloist, and by 1972 she was nominated a principal of the company. New York City Ballet's choreographers practically stood in line to create ballets for her. Balanchine himself gave her her first principal role with his new production of *Firebird* during the 1970 Stravinsky Festival. Robbins gave her roles in *The Goldberg Variations*, *An Evening's Waltzes*, *Four Bagatelles*, and *Scherzo Fantas-*

tique. John Clifford contributed roles in *Stravinsky Symphony in C* and *Tchaikovsky Suite No. 1*, and John Taras created *Song of the Nightingale* for her. In addition, her New York City Ballet repertory also included *Dances at a Gathering, The Cage, Concerto Barocco, Symphony in C, Tchaikovsky Pas de Deux,* and *Tarantella.*

Why did she defect? Kirkland has always been an individualist. Her father, Jack Kirkland, a playwright, who probably is best known for his adaptation of Erskine Caldwell's novel *Tobacco Road*, wanted his two daughters to become actresses. But first Johnna and later Gelsey found themselves moving toward dance. Gelsey Kirkland has always been something of a nonconformist, and her training has been strictly classical. She had a yearning to dance the major classic roles. She once said: "I don't think of myself as a star and I hope I never do. I left City Ballet because I wanted to dance the classics, ballets I had never danced before."

It was not quite as simple as that. One deciding factor was Mikhail Baryshnikov's asking her to dance with him in Ballet Theatre. He had seen her dance while the City Ballet was on tour in the Soviet Union, and at the same time, she had seen him at the Kirov. They both admired one another enormously, and Kirkland found the opportunity too great to turn down.

Kirkland joined American Ballet Theatre in the fall of 1974 and was instantly made a principal dancer, which is rare for new recruits. Her repertory with ABT has included virtually all of the major classics so far, with the exception of *Swan Lake.* Her partnership with Baryshnikov, particularly in *Giselle* and *La Sylphide*, has been exemplary, and she has found a place for herself not only in the classics, but also in the general Ballet Theatre repertory in works such as Tudor's *Shadowplay* and *Jardin aux Lilas* and Balanchine's *Theme and Variations.*

Kirkland is a unique American ballerina, with a style and manner all her own. She makes an admirable complement to Cynthia Gregory, rather in the way that Patricia McBride offers precisely the right contrast in City Ballet to Suzanne Farrell. So far her qualities have shown up most clearly in Romantic ballets, such as *Giselle* and *La Sylphide*, where her air of misty enchantment and total involvement leave an unforgettable impression. However, her first performances of Aurora in *The Sleeping Beauty* have suggested, as have her appearances in the *Don Quixote Pas de Deux*, a more crystalline and more purely classic style.

Ted Kivitt

Ted Kivitt is in many ways the epitome of the American male dancer. He started first tap dancing and later ballet classes for health reasons (as a boy he suffered from asthma), and he has become one of the most important male dancers of his generation. He was born in Miami, Florida, on December 21, 1942. His early training was with Alexander Gavrilov (the dancer who frequently substituted for Nijinsky in the Diaghilev Ballet) and Thomas Armour. During his early years he danced in night clubs and also became connected with the Miami Ballet, one of the country's many regional companies. In 1961, Ballet Theatre played in Miami, and Kivitt auditioned for the company. Six months later, he received a contract and came to New York.

Although he did not become a principal dancer until 1967, he was soon appearing in major roles. He emerged at a time when Ballet Theatre had an exceptional number of up and coming young male dancers, including Eliot Feld, William Glassman, Terry Orr, Paul Sutherland, and Edward Verso, but all of them, with the exception of Sutherland, who went first to the Harkness and later to the Joffrey, were *demi-caractère.* Kivitt was in effect the strongest classicist, and it was to him that the leading roles went.

Kivitt has always had an exceptionally strong technique. For example, in the leading role in Lander's *Etudes* in the finale he has been known to execute the phenomenal number of eight double *tours en l'air* without preparation. But it is not merely his technique that has placed him in the forefront of the company. His manly presence and essential nobility tinged with an unusual touch of friendliness have given his performances a character totally of their own. There is a particular honesty to his dancing that is most endearing and gives an edge to what otherwise might be a brilliant yet cold technique.

Kivitt has done virtually every classic leading role in the repertory and always with distinction. He never gives a bad performance, but occasionally pulls out an almost surprisingly brilliant one. It is a well-known and indeed much quoted fact that Kivitt feels underestimated by the company and occasionally resents the intrusion of guest artists upon what he considers his territory. He has no cause for fear. There is a specific American quality to Kivitt's dancing that is unmistakeable and is shared by such dissimilar dancers as Jacques d'Amboise and Edward Villella. Now approaching his mid-thirties, he probably has his best years ahead of him.

Natalia Makarova

Natalia Makarova is one of the great ballerinas of the twentieth century. She has a manner, a style, a finesse. She has also done a great deal for Ballet Theatre, with both its image and its popularity. She was born in Leningrad on October 21, 1940, and she grew up there in an apartment on Tchaikovsky Street near the river Neva. As a child she joined the Young Pioneers (an organization roughly equivalent to the Girl Scouts of America) and here she started to dance. Later, she joined the Vaganova School, the school that is officially attached to the Kirov Ballet, and she joined the company in 1959. On September 4, 1970, in London, during a season at the Royal Festival Hall, Makarova defected to the West.

The eleven years she spent with the Kirov were vitally important to her development as a dancer. Some time after her defection, Makarova said: "I shall never forget that the Kirov made me and I shall remain indebted to them the rest of my life."

I first saw Makarova dance in the summer of 1961 at the Royal Opera House, Covent Garden. The Kirov Ballet was paying its first visit to the West and had already mislaid Rudolf Nureyev in Paris. Now it came on to London. Makarova, although listed as a principal, was not one of the major stars, but she was permitted to dance her very first performance of Giselle during the London engagement. It was a sensation. There is a certain grace to certain debuts, and this was a debut that had more than a certain grace.

Makarova was always a nervy, sensitive dancer. Between her Covent Garden debut as Giselle and her defection, I recall quite a number of her performances: In Leningrad, she was marvelous in Anton Dolin's staging of Pas de Quatre; in Amsterdam,

she did a guest stint as Giselle with the Dutch National Ballet; and in London, she was able to perform before her sudden departure. She was always a developing dancer, getting better and better, and yet never quite fulfilled. Of course, her Giselle was splendid, but this apart, she somehow seemed on the brink of achievement.

Makarova left the Kirov, and indeed Russia, not for any political reason, but simply because she wanted to extend her repertory and increase her artistic range. After her decision to leave the Kirov, she naturally made enquiries, as she was in London, to see if there was a place for her with the Royal Ballet. There was not. She then accepted a contract with Ballet Theatre and remained with the company, as a full member, for two years. Her first performance was in New York on December 4, 1970, at the City Center 55th Street Theater. She danced Giselle, partnered by Ivan Nagy.

For a time she had an interesting partnership with Erik Bruhn, that was only broken by his premature retirement, and she also moved into Ballet Theatre's general repertory. She was particularly successful in the Tudor ballets, Dark Elegies, Pillar of Fire, Jardin aux Lilas, and Romeo and Juliet, where she was the most Botticelli-looking Juliet anyone could hope for. Her skills were developing and her genius was blossoming. Some of her performances both in Swan Lake and La Sylphide were remarkable even by then.

After two years she left the permanent roster of Ballet Theatre to become an international star. In 1972 she danced with Britain's Royal Ballet for the first time and set up a new partnership with Anthony Dowell. She also appeared with the Paris Opéra Ballet, La Scala de Milan, the Royal Danish Ballet, and the Ballet of the Berlin Opera. In April 1975, Makarova accepted an invitation from the Royal Ballet to become what was called a permanent guest artist. She accepted. Although she is now probably more with the British company than with Ballet Theatre—she and her husband have a house in London—she still dances quite frequently with ABT, and her visits are always eagerly awaited.

As a dancer she has something very special. Perhaps you could call it a passionate fragility; she is the kind of ballerina who makes almost every man in the audience want to take off his coat and place it protectingly around her shoulders. She is also very funny in soubrette roles. At times she can be too outrageous for comfort and too cheap for style, but mostly she is witty rather than humorous, and her dancing and characterizations are always presented with the flourish of enormous style.

In May 1974, Makarova did something different by mounting "The Kingdom of the Shades" scene from Petipa's *La Bayadère*. She worked very hard rehearsing the company, which gave its first triumphant performance of the ballet at the New York State Theater on July 3, 1974. The company danced excellently, yet to a very large extent their success was due to Makarova's patient and careful teaching.

Presumably in the future ABT will see rather less of Makarova than it has in the past, but she will always be welcome. She and the company were made for one another.

Ivan Nagy

Ivan Nagy was born in Debrecen, Hungary, on April 28, 1943. He started his ballet training with his mother, Viola Sarkozy, who was a well-known teacher in Hungary. At the age of seven he was accepted into the Ballet School of the Budapest Opera House, and he remained there for eight years before graduating into the Opera Ballet. Here, he was given many chances and danced in such works as *Gayane* and Leonid Lavrovsky's version of *Romeo and Juliet*. In 1965 he competed at the Varna Ballet Competition in Bulgaria, winning a silver medal.

One of the judges at Varna was Frederic Franklin, then director of the National Ballet in Washington, D.C. He invited Nagy to join the Washington company, and with the agreement of the Hungarian government, Nagy accepted. He stayed with the Washington company for three years, becoming the company's principal male dancer. For a season he was with New York City Ballet, but was given comparatively little to do except the last movement of Balanchine's *Symphony in C*. In 1968 he left City Ballet and joined Ballet Theatre as a soloist. A year later he was promoted to a principal.

With natural elevation, a noble style, and an effortless partnering ability, Nagy has become one of the world's greatest *premier danseurs*. He dances the entire classical repertory, but he is perhaps at his best in the romantic roles of James in *La Sylphide* and Albrecht in *Giselle*. He has danced with most of the ABT ballerinas, but his partnership with Natalia Makarova has probably been the most notable. It was Nagy who partnered her when she made her debut with the American company dancing *Giselle* on December 24, 1970, and they have danced together on many occasions since.

Although, since he joined the company, ABT has been Nagy's home base—he long ago decided to leave Hungary and settle in the United States—he appears with other companies all over the world. He is one of Margot Fonteyn's favorite partners, once doing an Australian tour with her and the Scottish Ballet.

Oddly enough, for such a distinguished dancer, Nagy has had comparatively few roles created for him. This is possibly because he is kept so busy in the classic repertory, and he is so firmly identified as the classic prince that he has very little time for anything else. Certainly he brings a great deal of life and conviction to these cardboard princes, which in itself makes him one of Ballet Theatre's most considerable assets.

Dennis Nahat

Of all the dancers with American Ballet Theatre, it is quite possible that Dennis Nahat is the most individualistic. He has a style and manner all his own.

Nahat was born in Detroit, Michigan, on February 2, 1946. He first studied with Enid Riordeau. Later in New York he studied at the Juilliard School and worked at the American Ballet Center, the official school of the Joffrey Ballet. In his early days in New York he took classes with Antony Tudor, Hector Zaraspe, José Limon, Mary Hinkson, Helen McGehee, and Bertram Ross. He made his debut in 1965 with the Joffrey Ballet but never left a particularly strong impression with this company. In 1968 he joined Ballet Theatre and things soon started to go well for him. He was appointed a principal dancer in 1973, and although he is not regularly with the company these days, he appears to be a kind of permanent guest artist and his appearances are always welcome.

His range is considerable, and although he has not got a virtuoso technique, it is good enough to encompass the role of The Third Sailor in *Fancy Free*. In other ballets he has run the gamut from Madge in *La Sylphide* to Alias in *Billy the Kid*. Roles that he has made particularly his own are the part Alvin Ailey created for him in *The River*, his brilliant characterization of The Devil in Agnes de Mille's *Three Virgins and a Devil*, and perhaps best of all The Dancing Master in Leonide Massine's *Gaîté Parisienne*. Before Nahat assumed the latter role it was thought of as a minor part, but he made it into something absolutely compelling. Later, he danced it at a Ballet Theatre gala and with the London Festival Ballet as a guest artist.

Nahat is also a choreographer, making his choreographic debut in 1969 with a ballet to Tchaikovsky called *Momentum*. Since then he has choreographed *Brahms Quintet* (first for the Royal Swedish Ballet in 1970, revived later the same year by ABT), *Ontogeny* (1970), *Mendelssohn Symphony* (1971—this was later revived by London Festival Ballet), and *Some Times* (1972). He has also choreographed for Broadway, including the Joseph Papp hit *Two Gentlemen of Verona*.

In recent years Nahat has spent more and more time in Cleveland, where his friend and former ABT colleague Ian Horvath runs a school and is the artistic director of the Cleveland Ballet, which gave its first fully professional performances during the 1976–77 season. Nahat is the company's associate director and will dance with the company and choreograph for it. In this premiere season, Nahat was scheduled to create *Suite Caracteristique* to Tchaikovsky, *Things Our Fathers Loved* to Charles Ives, and an untitled work to Chabrier, a *Grand Pas de Dix* to Glazunov, *Process* to music by Husa, and a revival of *Some Times*.

Terry Orr

Terry Orr was born in Berkeley, California, on March 12, 1943. He received his ballet training at the San Francisco Ballet School, chiefly with Lew Christensen. After seven years of study, he joined the San Francisco Ballet in 1959 and in 1962 was appointed a principal dancer. He appeared in most of the company's repertory, including *Con Amore*, *Jest of Cards*, *Divertissement d'Auber* and *The Nutcracker*. Indeed, Orr was so fully identified with the company that when the San Francisco Ballet made its Lincoln Center debut in 1965, his photograph was used as a company symbol in all its publicity. However, that same year Orr and his wife at that time, Cynthia Gregory, defected. After toying with the idea of auditioning for Balanchine, they chose Ballet Theatre. Orr was accepted instantly, but it took Gregory three auditions before Ballet Theatre would take her.

Orr was made a soloist in 1967 and promoted to a principal dancer in 1972. He is a natural *demi-caractère* dancer. He is a little short for princes, but he has a fine bearing and a strong, nervy technique. He dances Franz in *Coppélia* and Colin in *La Fille Mal Gardée*, but his major contribution to the repertory has been more in the area of character. He looks the all-American boy-next-door, a sort of balletic Andy Hardy, but his dancing has the strength of a natural classicist.

Probably his best roles have been as The Champion Roper in *Rodeo*, a boyishly psychopathic Billy in *Billy the Kid*, as the gangling, romantic The Second Sailor in *Fancy Free*, or as a fiercely tormented Petrouchka. He has danced many other leading roles, including leads in two Eliot Feld ballets, *Harbinger* and *At Midnight*, and nowadays is the company's first cast for the pure *demi-caractère* solo roles: the peasant *pas de deux* in *Giselle*, Benno (with the first act *pas de trois*) in *Swan Lake*, and Gurn (with a first act solo) in *La Sylphide*.

In recent years Orr has been appointed rehearsal assistant to the company, and clearly when the time comes for him to retire from active dancing he will assume more of this kind of responsibility.

Marcos Paredes

Marcos Paredes is one of the company's chief character dancers and also happens to be a member of the costume designer's union, and he works for the company in both capacities. He was born in Aguascalientes, Mexico, and he started his ballet training at the Academia de la Danza in Mexico City. He appeared with a number of Mexican companies, including the Ballet Contemporaneo and the Ballet Classico de Mexico. He first came to the United States to join the Denver Civic Ballet. He entered Ballet Theatre in 1965, became a soloist in 1968, and was appointed a principal dancer in 1973.

Paredes has a very intense, yet somehow friendly stage presence. It is a demeanor that has gone against his portrayal of The Young Man from the House Opposite in Tudor's *Pillar of Fire*, but it has also slowly enabled him to give a highly thought of performance of Hilarion in *Giselle*. He can be very funny as Widow Simone in *La Fille Mal Gardée*, and he has been effective in such varying roles as Madge in *La Sylphide*, The Moor in *Petrouchka*, and Tybalt in Tudor's *Romeo and Juliet*.

His costume credits have been very impressive. He has designed the costumes for *Gartenfest*, *Divertissement d'Auber*, *The Eternal Idol*, *Schubertiade*, *Times Past*, *Grand Pas Classique*, *Le Corsaire pas de deux*, *Flames of Paris pas de deux*, *Napoli divertissements*, *Apollo*, and *La Bayadère*.

John Prinz

Of all the dancers of ABT John Prinz is one of the most interesting. He is not just temperamental, he is positively moody (certainly earlier on in his career). But he has charm and enormous talent. He was born in Chicago on May 14, 1946. His uncle, a Yugoslav painter and actor, Tony Jackovich, persuaded his mother to send one of his sisters to dancing school. The young John went along and eventually the teacher, Russian dancer A. Comiakoff, talked him into taking class. A performance of *Giselle* with Alicia Alonso and Igor Youskevitch by Ballet Theatre in Chicago confirmed his ambition to be a dancer, and he studied further with two Chicago schools, both headed by Royal Ballet dancers, the first by Richard Ellis and his wife, Christine du Boulay, and the second, the now defunct Allegro School, led by Robert Lunnon and his wife, Doreen Tempest. In a sense this is why Prinz, with all his Slavic background and American training, often seems, oddly enough, an English dancer who would be perfectly at home with Britain's Royal Ballet.

When Prinz was sixteen he came to New York, turned up at Robert Joffrey's American Ballet Center, and asked for a scholarship. He got one. A year later he was accepted at the School of American Ballet, and in 1964 he was invited to join New York City Ballet. It was an exciting time, because it was just when City Ballet was moving into its new Lincoln Center home, the New York State Theater. In May of the following year, Prinz was given his very first solo role. In the *divertissement* in Balanchine's

new *Don Quixote*, Prinz was given the *pas de deux Mauresque* with Suki Schorer. It was one of the best episodes in the ballet, and it attracted immediate attention.

During the six years Prinz was with City Ballet he rose from the corps, to a soloist, to a principal. Balanchine created a lot of roles for him: the Valse Fantaisie in *Glinkiana* (injury prevented him from dancing the first performance), the *pas de trois* in the first act of *Jewels*, and the male lead in *La Source*. He danced many other roles in the City Ballet repertory, including *Tarantella*, *Four Temperaments* and *Western Symphony*, in the extraordinary virtuoso roles created for Edward Villella, and, most importantly, he re-created the role of Rimbaud in Frederick Ashton's *Illuminations*.

In 1969 Prinz married Nanette Glushak, then also a dancer with City Ballet. They left City Ballet and traveled to Europe, where John Cranko had suggested they might like to join his Stuttgart Ballet. They were unhappy in Stuttgart, suddenly left, returned to New York, and in 1970 joined ABT. Prinz joined as a soloist and was made a principal in 1972. Prinz's career in Ballet Theatre was proceeding splendidly: He partnered Makarova in her first modern role in the West (in Tudor's *Jardin aux Lilas*), he was Romeo in Tudor's *Romeo and Juliet*; he took the leads in such varied ballets as *Les Patineurs*, *The River*, *Etudes*, *Petrouchka*, *Fancy Free*, and *Les Sylphides*; and he danced a very successful Albrecht in Washington, D.C., to Diana Weber's *Giselle*, and everything looked rosy. Then there was an accident.

In the spring of 1974, American Ballet Theatre staged a new prduction by David Blair of the last act of Petipa's *The Sleeping Beauty*. It opened in Los Angeles in advance of its New York premiere. John Prinz danced the Bluebird on the first night. During the series of entrechats at the end of his variation, he broke his Achilles tendon. He was taken instantly to hospital.

This is one of the worst accidents that can happen to a dancer, although nowadays both surgery and remedial therapy are so advanced that some accidents that would have automatically ended a career in the past can now be overcome. Prinz was determined not to let a little thing like an Achilles tendon stop him. Gradually he has fought his way back. No, today he probably is not quite the dancer he would have been, but he is nevertheless very good and getting better. Each season he gets more of his technique back, and it could be that he will make a complete recovery. Prinz remains a fascinating dancer, and he has had to overcome a difficult handicap.

Marianna Tcherkassky

It seems as though Marianna Tcherkassky has always been with American Ballet Theatre. But she hasn't. She was born in 1953 in Glen Cove, New York. Her mother was a dancer and provided her with her earliest training. Later she went on a scholarship to the School of American Ballet. Her first professional engagements were with the André Eglevsky Company.

She joined Ballet Theatre in 1970, became a soloist in 1972, and was appointed a principal in 1976. Of partly Russian and partly oriental parentage she looks arresting, and her performances have just the right kind of elegance and personality. Tcherkassky has been increasingly evident in the repertory over the years, but probably the most headline-catching episode in her career was when through the illness of Gelsey Kirkland, Tcherkassky replaced her as Giselle. It was a striking debut, and she offers a great deal for the future.

Clark Tippet

When Clark Tippet was appointed a principal dancer of ABT in 1976 he was, at the age of twenty-two, the second youngest principal dancer ever appointed. (The youngest was Fernando Bujones.) He was born in Parsons, Kansas, but he began to study dance in New York City at Thalia Mara's National Academy of the Dance. He joined Ballet Theatre in 1972, he was made a soloist in 1975, and a year later he was advanced to principal. A beautiful partner, he has excelled in Glen Tetley's *Gemini* and, just for a difference, Rudolf Nureyev's *Raymonda*. Twyla Tharp created a special role for him in *Push Comes to Shove*, and he danced a leading role in the Tetley version of *Le Sacre du Printemps*.

Martine van Hamel

There are times when one is tempted to think that Martine van Hamel is not merely a dancer but a cult. She is indeed a dancer's dancer, a balletomane's dancer, a dancer for the cognoscenti and might be caviar to the general public. She is also gorgeous. She was born in Brussels on November 16, 1945, the daughter of a Dutch diplomat. Her early training was fragmented. Her father as a career diplomat went around the world, and Martine naturally followed. Therefore, her early training took place in Denmark, Holland, and Venezuela, before she finally settled down at the School of the National Ballet of Canada.

Although Van Hamel's early training sounds a trifle vague, it was not as indistinct as all that. For example, in Caracas she studied with Henry Danton from Britain's Royal Ballet from 1957 to 1959. When her father was transferred to Canada, she naturally went to the National Ballet School, which, again, is very much based on Royal Ballet lines. She joined the National Ballet of Canada in 1963 as a soloist. In 1966, partnered by the Canadian dancer Earl Kraul, she won a gold medal at the International Ballet Competition in Varna, Bulgaria. She returned to Canada as a heroine, but soon became bored.

She was a principal dancer by now, dancing most of the classic leads, including The Ballerina in *La Bayadère* and Odette/Odile in Erik Bruhn's version of *Swan Lake*. She was very fine in a widely spaced repertory—including Balanchine's *Concerto Barocco*, Kenneth MacMillan's *Solitaire*, and Tudor's *Jardin aux Lilas*. In 1968 she went as a guest artist to the Royal Swedish Ballet, and in 1970 she joined the Joffrey Ballet. It was an unhappy time. She had hardly anything to do. Later that year she went into the corps de ballet of Ballet Theatre. She had never danced in a corps de ballet in her life, but settled down to the experience. In 1971 she became a soloist, and two years later she was a principal.

She has now danced most of the leading roles in the repertory and is particulary regarded for her performances in *Swan Lake*, *La Sylphide*, and *Raymonda*. She has a creamy, expansive style and is one of the great contemporary ballerinas. She also has an occasional weight problem—she is a big woman, which happens to be one of her unexpected charms as a ballerina, a profession where daintiness is all too often the rule. Yet the important thing is how beautifully she moves. She has a very special grace to her. Which is why I suppose, to people who care about the flaunting eloquence of dance, Van Hamel is not merely a dancer but a cult.

Charles Ward

Charles Ward was born in Los Angeles, California, on October 24, 1952. He graduated from high school there while training with Stanley Holden and Gene Marianaccio at the Los Angeles School of Dance. He came to New York and worked with the American Ballet Theatre School and Maggie Black. He danced briefly with the Houston Ballet before joining the corps de ballet of ABT in the fall of 1972. Two years later he was made a soloist, and in 1976 he was promoted a principal of the company.

Ward is a brilliant technician and seemingly a born *premier danseur*. He has excelled in roles such as the leads in *Etudes* and *Theme and Variations* and has also proved exceptional in Glen Tetley's *Gemini*.

Sallie Wilson

Of all the dancers of American Ballet Theatre, Sallie Wilson is one of the most interesting. She has a very special manner and a very unusual style. She has a strong classic technique—in her earlier days she was lovely in pure classic *pas de deux*—but she chose the role of dramatic ballerina, and she has become America's most noted dramatic ballerina since Nora Kaye.

She was born in Fort Worth, Texas, April 18, 1932. Her first teacher was Dorothy Colter Edwards, but when she came to New York it was first and foremost Margaret Craske, then also, particularly when she became one of the prime exponents of his ballets, Antony Tudor. She also took classes with Edward Caton. She first joined Ballet Theatre in 1949. There were various gaps in her relationship with the company after that. She was with the Metropolitan Opera Ballet, with Tudor, for some time, and later she had two interesting seasons with Balanchine's New York City Ballet. On May 14, 1959, she had the fascinating experience of appearing with Martha Graham and Bertram Ross in the first part of the Graham/Balanchine collaboration *Episodes*. She was Mary, Queen of Scots.

When Ballet Theatre reformed she rejoined the company, and in 1961 she was made a principal. She had enjoyed working with Balanchine, but it appeared that there was no future in the relationship for either of them.

Nowadays with Ballet Theatre, Wilson has been primarily concerned with the Tudor repertory—she even staged an outrageously awful production of Tudor's *Gala Performance* for the company at the Brooklyn Academy of Music—but her major parts have been in *Pillar of Fire*, in *Dark Elegies*, and, away from Tudor for a moment, in Agnes de Mille's *Fall River Legend*. She has also been excellent in De Mille's *Three Virgins*, and Robbins created a special and very touching role for her in *Les Noces*.

Gayle Young

Gayle Young was born in Lexington, Kentucky, and he did not begin ballet classes until he was attending the University of California at Berkeley. It was then he took classes with Dorothy Pring. When he came to New York he attended the American Ballet Theatre School. He danced with both the Robert Joffrey Ballet and New York City Ballet, and then he joined the Broadway musical *Redhead*, starring Gwen Verdon and Richard Kiley. It was during the run of this musical, in 1960, that Young was invited to join American Ballet Theatre. He accepted and was named a principal dancer in 1964.

As a very secure partner, Young never had quite the classic technique to make a *premier danseur*. Yet he has been very useful to the company in numerous character roles. His performance of The Man She Must Marry, for example, in Tudor's *Jardin aux Lilas* is a model of emotional economy, and he brings the same warm, yet dispassionate approach to The Young Pastor in *Fall River Legend*.

Alicia Alonso

There is no way in which one can consider Alicia Alonso a member of American Ballet Theatre. And yet there is no way in which one can not consider Alicia Alonso a member of American Ballet Theatre. She was with the company almost from the beginning, and despite a period when she defected to the Ballet Russe de Monte Carlo, she retained her connection until the Castro revolution in her native Cuba in 1959. She then became the director of the Cuban National Ballet, and for many years was persona non grata in the United States.

She was born in Havana, Cuba, and her age has always been something of a mystery. Horst Koegler's *Friedrichs Ballettlexikon* (normally very accurate on such matters) suggests, indeed boldly states, her birthdate as May 22, 1917, which, if anyone is counting, would make her two years older than Margot Fonteyn. The date does not seem unlikely.

Until politics intervened, her relationship with Ballet Theatre was always close. She created the ballerina role in Balanchine's *Theme and Variations*, and, oddly enough, through the illness of Nora Kaye, she was the first person to dance The Accused in Agnes de Mille's *Fall River Legend*. Her performance in *Giselle* became one of the best known of her generation. She came back to New York during the summer of 1975 when she danced, most triumphantly, during the company's 35th Anniversary Gala. A year later she came back for a series of performances in the title role of Alberto Alonso's *Carmen Suite*. It is a bad ballet but a great performance. Alonso will always have a special place in the hearts of American ballet lovers.

Family Album

Olga Spessivtzeva, Anton Dolin, Lucia Chase, and Ferdnand Nault watching a studio rehearsal.

David Blair rehearsing Ted Kivitt and Cynthia Gregory in Blair's staging of act 3 of *The Sleeping Beauty*, 1974.

Cynthia Gregory and Ivan Nagy rehearsing the *pas de deux* from *Apollo*.

ARKS

ARKS

Antony Tudor rehearsing Richard Cammack, John Sowinski, and Bojan Spassoff.

At *left*, Erik Bruhn rehearsing Cynthia Gregory and Ivan Nagy in Bruhn's staging of *La Sylphide*. And Eliot Feld rehearsing Paula Tracy, Sallie Wilson, and Daniel Levins in Feld's *The Soldier's Tale*.

André Eglevsky rehearsing Paolo Bortoluzzi and Carla Fracci in *Le Spectre de la Rose*.

Gelsey Kirkland in rehearsal.

Natalia Makarova and Anthony Dowell rehearsing *Swan Lake* for the 1976 gala.

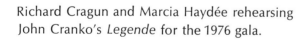
Richard Cragun and Marcia Haydée rehearsing John Cranko's *Legende* for the 1976 gala.

Natalia Makarova in a *La Sylphide* rehearsal.

Natalia Makarova, John Prinz, Carla Fracci, and Ivan Nagy in *Romeo and Juliet*.

JACK MITCHELL

Cynthia Gregory, Keith Lee, Sallie Wilson, and Ivan Nagy rehearsing *The River*.

Karena Brock with the wardrobe mistress.

ARKS

Carla Fracci in her dressing room.

Natalia Makarova and Fernando Bujones. A pledge to friendship, Russian style.

Galas

LOUIS PÉRES

An excerpt from *Fancy Free* with Terry Orr, Jerome Robbins, John Kriza, and Harold Lang at the Thirty-fifth Anniversary Gala, January 1975.

Marianna Tcherkassky and Fernando Bujones in *The Nutcracker* for the
Thirty-fifth Anniversary Gala, January 1975.

DINA MAKAROVA

André Eglevsky and Igor Youskevitch partnering Cynthia Gregory in the "Rose Adagio" from *Princess Aurora*, staged by Anton Dolin for the Thirty-fifth Anniversary Gala, January 1975.

Rudolf Nureyev and Gelsey Kirkland in the *Corsaire pas de deux* at the July 1975 gala.

Erik Bruhn, Cynthia Gregory, and Rudolf Nureyev in Bournonville's *La Ventana pas de trois* at the July 1975 gala.

BIL LEIDERSDORF

Alicia Alonso's triumphant return to Ballet Theatre at the July 1975 gala in the act 2 *pas de deux* from *Swan Lake* with Jorge Esquivel.

Mikhail Baryshnikov and Twyla Tharp in Tharp's *Once More, Frank*.

Martine van Hamel and Peter Breuer in the *Corsaire pas de deux*, August 1976 gala.

Left to Right: Noella Pontois, Mikhail Baryshnikov, Rudolf Nureyev, Cynthia Gregory, Erik Bruhn, Alicia Alonso, Jorge Esquivel, Ivan Nagy, Eleanor D'Antuono, and Gelsey Kirkland at the July 1975 gala.

LOUIS PÉRES

Cynthia Gregory and Erik Bruhn in *Miss Julie* at the Thirty-fifth Anniversary Gala, January 1975.

Alicia Alonso and Jorge Esquivel in *Carmen*, 1976.

Lynn Seymour in Sir Frederick Ashton's *Homage to Isadora*.

Gelsey Kirkland and Ivan Nagy in Kenneth MacMillan's *Romeo and Juliet*.
© 1976; from *Waldman on Dance, William* Morrow & Co., 1977, by permission.

MAX WALDMAN

LOUIS PÉRES

Natalia Makarova in a curtain call after a *Swan Lake* performance at the Kennedy Center.

Cynthia Gregory is given a paper throw after *Swan Lake*.

DINA MAKAROVA

Alicia Alonso, Lucia Chase, and Clive Barnes at a reception.

Aaron Copland shakes hands with John Kriza after a performance of *Billy the Kid* at the White House in the presence of the late President and Mrs. John F. Kennedy.

Anthony Tudor and
Mrs. William Zeckendorf, Jr.

STEPHANIE RANÇOU

LOUIS PÉRES

Nora Kaye, John Kriza, and Rudolf Nureyev.